H

The Massey Lectures

The Massey Lectures are co-sponsored by CBC Radio, House of Anansi Press, and Massey College, in the University of Toronto. The series was created in honour of the Right Honourable Vincent Massey, former governor general of Canada, and was inaugurated in 1961 to enable distinguished authorities to communicate the results of original study on subjects of contemporary interest.

This book comprises the 2002 Massey Lectures, "Beyond Fate," broadcast in November 2002 as part of CBC Radio's *Ideas* series. The producer of the series was Philip Coulter; the executive producer was Bernie Lucht.

Margaret Visser

Margaret Visser was born in South Africa, studied at the Sorbonne, and received her doctorate in classics from the University of Toronto. She is the author of four bestselling books: *The Geometry of Love*, finalist for the Charles Taylor Prize; *Much Depends on Dinner*, winner of the Glenfiddich Prize for Food Book of the Year; *The Rituals of Dinner*, winner of the International Association of Culinary Professionals' Literary Food Writing Award and the Jane Grigson Award in the US; and *The Way We Are*, a collection of essays. She divides her time among Toronto, Barcelona, and southwestern France.

Also by Margaret Visser

Much Depends on Dinner
The Rituals of Dinner
The Way We Are
The Geometry of Love

BEYOND FATE

Margaret Visser

ANANSI

Published in 2002 by
House of Anansi Press Inc.
110 Spadina Ave., Suite 801
Toronto, ON, M5V 2K4
Tel. 416-363-4343
Fax 416-363-1017
www.anansi.ca

Distributed in Canada by
Publishers Group Canada
250A Carlton Street
Toronto, ON, M5A 2L1
Tel. 416-934-9900
Toll free order numbers:
Tel. 800-663-5714
Fax 800-565-3770

CBC logo used by permission

06 05 04 03 02   2 3 4 5

National Library of Canada Cataloguing in Publication Data

Visser, Margaret, 1940–
Beyond fate / Margaret Visser.

(CBC Massey lectures series)
Includes bibliographical references.
ISBN 0-88784-679-3

1. Humanities. I. Title. II. Series.

AC8.V46 2002   001.3   C2002-904012-4

Cover design: Bill Douglas at The Bang
Typesetting: Colborne Communications

Printed and bound in Canada

The Canada Council | Le Conseil des Arts
FOR THE ARTS | DU CANADA
SINCE 1957 | DEPUIS 1957

*We acknowledge for their financial support of our publishing
program the Canada Council for the Arts, the Ontario Arts
Council, and the Government of Canada through the Book
Publishing Industry Development Program (BPIDP).*

for Megan and Miriam

Contents

... in my nightly visions the mysterious precept, "Upward, not Northward," haunts me like a soul-devouring Sphinx.
                                        —- Edwin Abbott Abbott, *Flatland*

ACKNOWLEDGEMENTS

MY THANKS ARE FIRST OF ALL to my husband, Colin, with whom I have hammered out, discussed, questioned, and reconsidered every argument in this book. I also remember with gratitude the many students I taught at York University in Toronto; they helped me to see the relevance of the ancient ways of thinking to modern life. The year I spent at Regis College and the Lonergan Research Institute provided me with plenty of matter for reflection, as well as opportunities for insight. I want to thank especially Richard Handler, my producer for many years on CBC's *Morningside*, not only for his professional skill but for many hours of stimulating conversation on this subject and others related to it. I would also like to thank Martha Sharpe at House of Anansi Press, from whom I received first-class editing, my copy editor, Janice Weaver, and Philip Coulter, the CBC producer of the Massey Lectures.

I

DRAWING A LINE

ONE OF THE PROUDEST ACHIEVEMENTS of modernity is its investment in freedom of every kind, personal, moral, and economic. At our most hopeful — and most arrogant — we feel that being modern means having arrived at a point where constraint can be routed, or at least reduced as far as possible. Overweening we may be about this, but we do, in the cultures of the Mediterranean, Europe, America, and their derivatives, have reason to be respectful of the advances made in achieving freedom, beginning with the abatement of fate, and also of chance, disorder, and randomness. For more than two thousand years we have fought for freedom from fate, and in many ways we have attained it. However, we seem, in important respects, now to be letting that freedom slip from our grasp. Fatalism and submission to chance, within modernity itself, is at present gaining ground. We are falling back into fate. In order to consider how and why this is happening, I want to look at the assumptions that derive from ancient metaphorical models of fate — images that are very much with us today.

Metaphors occur constantly in our speech, even if we are not being especially poetic. "You look luscious," we might say; or, "I'm a chocoholic"; or, "The bottom line is ..." Moribund phrases, or at least blunted by use as all of these are, they still reveal attitudes of mind — in these cases, the desire to consume, even if the item is another person; an acceptance that greed, while naughty, is not only nice but lightly to be accepted as addictive ("addictive" itself now has a clichéd sense, meaning merely desirable or favourite); and a belief that the deepest decisions in life are a matter of totting up advantages and disadvantages as though they were figures in a sum, with the total as "the bottom line." Metaphors make connections between things not normally thought of in the same breath; being vivid and concrete, living metaphors arouse attention. They entertain; they give us images with which to think. But just because they can be pleasant and useful, metaphoric models can deceive; if carelessly used, they can unobtrusively, and therefore insidiously, lead our thinking astray.

For example, for hundreds of years people have kept chickens in coops or allowed them to run free near their houses; the birds were constantly under the eyes of their owners. People reflected upon the behaviour of chickens and then decided that it resembled that of human beings in various respects. Henpecking was interesting — a phenomenon that could be related to human bullying. So was the fact that cocks — never hens — ruled the roost. They crowed; hens merely clucked. Is it not the case, then, that men ought to speak up and women ought to keep quiet?

Once the hen-run had become a "self-evident" metaphoric model for human groups and families, the behaviour of chickens could reflect back what had been projected onto it, so as to reinforce human conventions and social prejudices. A Victorian gentleman, like a rooster, ruled his household. Again like a cock, he often felt it to be his right to take his pick from among his female servants for sexual favours. A worthy wife was not only quiet, modest, submissive, and thrifty, but also in need of protection and as easily pleased as a barnyard hen. And so forth.[1]

The phrase "the survival of the fittest" was first used by the social theorist Herbert Spencer to describe the social and economic process in which weak rivals are eliminated by strong ones in the course of commercial competition. Existing social hierarchies were, he believed, "natural" and hence immutable. In editions of *On the Origin of Species* subsequent to the book's first appearance in 1859, the phrase was taken up by Charles Darwin and applied to his theory of evolution by natural selection.[2] Applying human capitalist activity — what is called the "law" of the marketplace — to genetic and environmental shifts made natural selection seem like an entirely different concept: that of an intentional struggle for profit on the part of each plant or animal.[3] As in our reading of the behaviour of chickens, a view of human nature is projected onto the natural world. The process is then reversed, and the expropriation by some people of other people's resources is validated as "natural" and, therefore, inevitable.

Although Karl Marx saw clearly that Darwin was projecting social perceptions onto the animal world,[4] he nevertheless thought that Darwin's theory of conflict as an evolutionary principle confirmed his own view of class conflict as the key to social change. All this occurred because of the reading into emergent probabilities in nature a metaphor that had been derived from *social* exploitation. Nor has social Darwinism gone away. It has been revived recently in an especially aggressive guise, even as hard capitalism finds itself once again the king of the castle, all opposition apparently routed.

We have, then, to watch our metaphors. This is not to say, however, that we should get rid of the practice of creating and using them. For metaphors partake of art; they make people "see" what is being talked about. A metaphor can put an interlocutor right inside the author's mind, making the reader or listener active and complicit in the process of communication. Metaphors make writing and talking *interesting*. The word "interest" originally meant "is among": *inter-est*. Consider Shakespeare's lines:

> And this our life, exempt from public haunt,
> finds tongues in trees, books in the running brooks,
> sermons in stones, and good in every thing.[5]

Some flat-footed editor (or perhaps a tired actor) is said to have corrected these lines, which he perceived as being merely mixed up. "*Leaves* in trees," he insisted, "*stones* in the running brooks," and "sermons in *books*." How obvious, how flat, can you get? No brightness there — no life, no *interest*. And therefore, no insight. Shakespeare makes us feel that the world is a totality, all of it interconnected; his poetry compels us to join him in seeing the connections. "Common sense," which here severs the links, also denies us the insight.

Having heavily subscribed to the use of metaphors and metaphorical models, and having delivered a warning about them, I want in these chapters to consider a set of interlocking metaphors, a metaphorical model, ancient but still ubiquitous, with an influential reach of which we are only rarely fully conscious. In these metaphors, time is expressed in terms of space. Spatialized time then encourages us to see events as inevitable, as fated.

Imagine, then, a line drawn on a blank page. Time can seem to us to resemble such a line, especially if we see or imagine the line in the process of being drawn. This image, unspoken, a common currency taken utterly for granted, underlies many of our assumptions about time, and even the grammar of most — and possibly all — languages.

Space is not effortlessly perceived by us as value-free; the human body sees to that. We have, for example, a front and a back. Our senses, with the exception of touch, are all located in front; even our ear passages are positioned so that we hear better what is in front of us than what is behind. We normally move forwards, or "ahead." The word shows us that heads are presumed to be in front, not only for four-footed animals, where they obviously lead the body, but for people, where they sit on top. People who head others are above them. We find it good, metaphorically as well as practically, to move forwards, and we need strong reasons before we will agree to backtrack. We stand erect on our two legs, so our own posture makes verticality desirable and even uplifting to us: up is mostly better than down.

Only when spatial knowledge and spatial words are in place do children begin to express relations in time, which are harder to grasp — and far more slippery thereafter. The language itself makes spatial words express temporal concepts — imitating the order in which a child learns, and in doing so perhaps assisting the child to learn to speak. Events, we say, "take place"; we think of them and the connections among them by means of images.

Time is most commonly thought of as a line along which events move as though they were separate objects. Moments in time come to resemble trucks moving along a highway or logs being carried down a river. "Road" time stands still, and occurrences move along it; "river" time, on the other hand, itself flows along or rolls by. If we picture ourselves standing on a riverbank, on a road, or on the verge of one, an event seems to approach us from farther down the line. It comes to pass; in English, we again give away the metaphorical nature of our thinking by saying, afterwards, that such an event is "past." An event that is here and now is "present," like a pupil present in class. We also speak of the coming months and the years gone by. We look forward to dessert if we expect to have any. Wittgenstein pointed out that we live in the past or we live in London: the grammar is the same.[6]

When we make gestures, we trace lines in the air with our hands to render our ideas expressive. Even our thoughts seem to us to follow pathways, to make connections. Gestures leave no marks, however, so when we want to make a complex point, and to be clearly understood, we find ourselves actually drawing patterns on the ground or on paper or a blackboard. These are metaphorical lines, referring to a spatial model for dimensional or temporal or even more abstract concepts. The model is useful precisely because we can count on it that other people will understand it immediately and remember it better than they would most merely verbal accounts. Diagrams are striking. The lines and spaces instantly appeal to the pictorial model of time and causal progression that we so easily fetch up from our minds; this lends such pictures the power to "speak more than a thousand words."

A lecturer attempting to express time to an audience is very likely to draw it, on a blackboard, say, as a line, with perhaps an X or an arrowhead marking the spot that is the present moment. After that, he may add a line of dots. The line shows the past, solid because known; the dots indicate what lies ahead, in the largely unknown (therefore spotty) future. The model implies movement along a road, and the arrowhead gives us the direction. (The road, of course, would most naturally move from left to right, the reason being that our own culture has decided, entirely arbitrarily, that we must write from left to right — not right to left, or up and down, as in some other scripts.)

One of the things such a picture means is that the past,

once it has happened, cannot be altered. And yet, the very fact that time has become a picture of a road suggests to us that we could conceivably travel in both directions, as we could along a road. Why should we not be able to live backwards, just as we might, for instance, stop a car and then reverse it down the road again? Why should we not be able to remember forwards rather than only backwards? The idea of our reversing along the road of life invites us to think of a future that again resembles the past, in that it cannot be altered. Such a future is laid down, like a road: it is fated.

In *Through the Looking-Glass*, the White Queen explains to Alice that behind the mirror, time can go either way.

"I don't understand you," said Alice. "It's dreadfully confusing!"

"That's the effect of living backwards," the Queen said kindly; "it always makes one a little giddy at first."

"Living backwards!" Alice repeated in great astonishment. "I never heard of such a thing!"

"— but there's one great advantage in it, that one's memory works both ways."

"I'm sure *mine* only works one way," Alice remarked. "I can't remember things before they happen."

"It's a poor sort of memory that only works backwards," the Queen remarked.

"What sort of things do *you* remember best?" Alice ventured to ask.

"Oh, things that happened the week after next," the Queen replied in a careless tone.[7]

A road, of course, remains after the traveller has passed over it, like a road on a map. Actually performing the drawing of a line on a blackboard in itself takes time, so the teacher is probably reminding the students that time, in our experience, always marches on or passes. But the drawing remains, as time never does. Time, in such a drawing, appears to exist on its own, without anyone (in the picture) experiencing it — as though an activity could be performed without a performer. This, as we shall see, is a common mistake made whenever diagrams, either actual or imaginary, are used to express not only time but moral issues, or profitability, or any kind of social arrangement. The metaphor is useful: it enables us, for example, to analyse, to measure, and to count. But the metaphor must be carefully and consciously kept in its place. Time's existence as a line, isolated from anyone or anything living in time, is as impossible as divorcing the shape of an orange from its colour, its juiciness, or its taste.

Picturing time, or life's "journey," as a line or a road can illustrate what it feels like to make a choice. Choice is thought of as arrival at a crossroads: confronted with two or more possible avenues, the traveller embarks on one; the others are roads not taken.[8] When this picture is used to describe choice, the road not taken continues to exist on the page, as a real road remains but a series of events that have not taken place cannot. Subsequent choices are represented by further bifurcating lines. This diagram is sometimes referred to as "tree time." It is misleading because all the possibilities, now gone because not chosen, appear to remain, just as the branches of a tree reach to its budding tips. The same picture can also be used for a different purpose entirely: to illustrate the various ramifications (literally "branchings," keeping the tree metaphor) of the decisions we make. In this case, all of the outcomes represented really do take place; the lines stand for the various real consequences of the action in question. But the picture, whether it depicts things that happen or things that do not happen, is the same.

The diagram, again, depends on the idea of maps and journeys. Important turning points in our lives are perceived as moments when we reached the crossroads: a person walking the road of life comes to a place where one direction becomes two; this is the depiction of a choice. In the folklore of all races, crossroads are among the most uncanny of places. All kinds of ghosts, monsters, and underworld gods haunt them; gibbets are placed there, and nowhere is more propitious for magical processes designed to predict the future.[9] Stories abound where, in the course of a journey, a choice between roads becomes immensely significant in the fate of the traveller. One such "turning point" began with the reaction of the Greek hero Oedipus, proud and swift to anger, when a stranger met him on his route and threatened to force him off the road. He slew the man, whom he much later discovered was his father, at the very specific "place where the three roads meet." With that, he thought he was free. In fact, he found himself travelling, hindered no longer, down the road — the fated road — to Thebes. There he would fulfil the second part of the oracle that had predicted he would kill his father and marry the widowed queen, his mother.[10]

Ancient Greeks thought a great deal about fate, and when they did, the metaphors they used to think with were often spatial, indeed geometrical. The Greeks were obsessed with geometry. Among the first traces of them that we possess are their pots in the style called Geometric,[11] after its most obvious characteristic, the geometrical patterns drawn on the curved clay surfaces. Several hundred years later, by which time Greek thinkers — leaning heavily upon mathematical interpretations of religious ideas and religious interpretations of mathematics — had permanently altered the intellectual history of the world, we find Plato writing over the gateway to his Academy, "Let no one enter here who does not know geometry." Fate, for them, was a spatial and diagrammatic idea from the beginning. It was a gigantic blueprint, a "design" laid out in advance. A tendency to lean on linear metaphors continues both to inspire and to haunt our imaginations today. We need think only of the signs of the zodiac and their interpretation in astrology, or of palmistry, the reading of people's characters and fates from the lines on the palms of their hands. Geometrical metaphors in general can predispose us, when we are being careless, to cage up our vision and fail to let go of fatalism. I'll be giving in the course of this book lots of modern examples of the fatal diagram.

In traditional poetry, a person's life has often been imagined as a line representing time: a thread spun by the gods, by fate, or by the three Fates. In Greek, the names of these relentless mythical crones were Clotho (Spinner), Lachesis (Allotment), and Atropos (Not to be Turned Aside). They indicated past, present, and future: the past as already spun and purely linear; the present an intersection, station, or point marked out upon the line; the future as what you think you can control but cannot. Roman, Scandinavian, and Germanic mythologies also knew three Fates. They spun or braided the ropes of events in world history. They also made individual fates for human beings, in parallel with a life, the thread starting at its beginning and being snipped off when the time came to die. Or the fate was complete from the beginning, and it remained only for the person to travel his or her allotted span, the "road" of life. The three witches in *Macbeth* are versions of the Fates. Shakespeare, however, insists on his characters' free will: the riddling fiends mislead, but they never force decisions.[12]

What the myths of fate express is the sense we all have at times that we are not in charge; that events, rules, and systems act upon us, or make us act, in ways not of our choosing. It is entirely right that we should realize this, but we have to discriminate between what is in fact changeable and what is not. The diagram metaphor — its very clarity, its self-evidence — leans heavily on the side of inalterability, of the hopelessness of change.

The idea of fate as a thread or a rope makes one's fate into a thing, a lifespan applied to but separate from the person who has to live it, like the road a person cannot but walk. Fate is bestowed like an object, a "given": stories tell of the three Fates being invited to a baby's birth, or a naming ceremony, or a wedding, and bringing gifts that constitute the fate of the receiver.[13] A painful fate is like the Bed of Procrustes; he was a cruel bandit who forced his victims to lie on his bed, relentlessly chopping or stretching them so they would fit it. Crucifixion was a punishment, invented by ancient Greeks and adopted by Romans, in which a human being was nailed to a vertical, wooden, man-shaped fate.

A line, like a life, has a beginning and an end. Death comes to all of us, as birth was our beginning, and fate is always closely identified with these two — with death especially. A line has two ends. Being points, these ends are different things in kind from the distance connecting them. Yet the ends of lines cannot be subtracted from the lines; one end cannot be unless the other exists. Now, if you picture the line of life as flexible — a rope or thread, say, rather than a line already drawn on paper — you might take the two ends of it and join them. You will have created another thing entirely: an area. The diagram representing time has become two-dimensional.

On paper, the area inside a periphery is made of the same stuff as that outside it, but the line turns the inner area into something different. The outline gives space a shape, concentrating it until it is mysteriously "more" than the undifferentiated area outside the boundary.[14] Once this line has been drawn, life can be thought of as either an area or a line. Carl Gustav Jung, for instance, imagined the self as a circle that one "circumambulates" in the course of living.[15] Jung also described a reverse movement that begins in mid-life, as the self moves into

integration and begins to pursue the inner life, simplifica-
tion, limitation, intensification, and what he called
"individual culture": it is coming home to the starting
point, finishing the encircling life-journey, completing the
self.[16]

The line — here an outline — is a human life lived in
time, with all its peripeties; of course, when it is a picture
of the twists and turns, the vicissitudes, of a human existence, it will never give a purely circular shape to the area
within. Life as an area expresses something quite different. Here no time, no movement, is expressed. Instead,
we see ourselves as bounded, limited, with a wall around
us, giving shape and definition to who we are. The wall is
made up of circumstances — the word means literally
"things standing in a ring around" — seeming to enclose,
indeed to create, a human self. But the outline is also created in the course of living, out of events and the actions
we perform: the picture says that we are what we do.
Outlines are always in some sense at odds with the areas
they enclose: they keep what is inside from escaping. As
Samuel Beckett once put it, "The whiskey bears a grudge
against the decanter."[17]

The outline is a "boundary" — a word that may be
related to binding: the rope metaphor easily returns. Such
an outline may imprison or protect: once again, the diagram can say very different things, and we have to be
aware which we mean. A boundary is like a fence demar-
cating a piece of land. (When we talk of a person's "lot" in
life, we should recall that a "lot" can also mean an area,
such as a parking "lot.") Until very recent times, people

would immediately have pictured a city wall, built with enormous skill and energy in order to protect the area inside it from enemies. It might be a house wall or a suit of armour, protecting like a shell the vulnerable human being depicted as the area inside. How terrible for this outline to be broken — like a city with its walls breached and lying open to its foes or a warrior pierced by a weapon or even cut in two, beheaded, dismembered. From an enemy's point of view, of course, breaking that boundary, dividing that area, is a glorious feat. It all depends on who is using the diagram.

In the Western world, the metaphor of the ideally inviolable area allotted to each person is daily embodied in table settings. Each diner sits on an upright, separate chair drawn up to a table on which is laid his or her "place." This is an area bounded by metal slicing, piercing, dipping, and digging instruments, or cutlery: the knife, the fork, the spoon, and sometimes more than one of each. The plate with food on it is round — an unbroken ring, holding the diner's portion. We also speak of a person's lot or fate as his or her "portion" in life.

The table represents the group; its edge is the group's outline. A table, like a diagram, stresses both togetherness among the insiders, the ones given places and portions, and exclusion of those not asked: distinction and rejection or relegation to outside. People who have been "well brought up" (remember that higher is better) will not help themselves to other people's food; they will not lean into other people's areas, stick out their elbows, rest their elbows on the table (since that would necessarily mean occupying space outside their previously demarcated areas), or stretch their arms across the spaces imagined as an invisible dome over every individual's place.

This separateness at the table, like the table itself, is highly specific to our own culture — and a relatively recent achievement.[18] It took centuries to develop, and enormous amounts of effort and constraint went into its elaboration. Behind it lies the diagram of fate as separate portions, and three times a day, dinner ensures that the ideas it represents are dramatized. We had to invent plates; to force people never to touch the food with their hands; to create forks, change the shapes of knives, and insist that people not point with the cutlery. All this artificiality was felt to be worth the effort, in part because it supported the embodiment of that image of ourselves as bounded areas: we were slowly becoming more and more individualistic.

Table manners, which differ from culture to culture, are always a *convention* — literally, in Latin, a "coming together" — a series of rules people create, and agree to respect and keep. Table manners, in our own case, control how people eat; they also cover the order of courses in a dinner, from hors d'oeuvres to dessert — but they never decide who is to be invited, what people are actually going to eat, or what they will talk about while eating. If we look at a table set for dinner, the guests are ideas, the occupants of places laid out for them. But when we sit down on the chairs and start to eat and drink and talk, the thinness of the description of human beings as diagrammatical spaces becomes evident. We are real and rounded human beings, enacting our lives in intense relationship with other people — even as we agree, having come together, to keep our behaviour within perfectly artificial bounds.

Two mistakes are revealed by careless use of the ubiquitous metaphorical diagram in this context. We often forget that people are much more than bounded and protected, self-sufficient and unrelated individuals, statistical data, players of roles, counters in the making of deals. We may also forget that good manners are not morality. They force the mannerly temporarily to imitate morality, but they are not in themselves moral, for manners may be impeccable yet remain a mere façade. Both concepts, individualism and mannerliness, are basic, useful, desirable, even essential. But they are only a beginning, only single aspects of what it is to be human; they are never enough.

We often need to be reminded that when we think of ourselves — our dinner tables, our lives — as areas bounded by lines, we have silently left out the *time* element. People at table only rarely change places: a table setting does not allow for travelling. However, the structure of the world has expressed time for us as movement in space, from the beginning. Days are the recurrent passage of the sun across the sky; nights occupy the time when the sun is out of sight on its law-abiding quotidian round, while the moon takes its turn and moves across the expanse of starry darkness over us. Years and months are movements in space of sun and moon, accompanied by recurring lunar changes, or phases. Nature is cyclic; tides rise and fall and seasons change in regular sequence, in tune with the trajectories of sun and moon.

Circles may turn or stand still, so circles can introduce the idea of movement into our spatial metaphors for time. *Kyklos* is Greek for a circle or for anything round, including a crowd standing in a ring, a family circle, a circle of acquaintances. It also means a wheel, the function of which is to turn — as in the modern word "bicycle." In English, *circles* may well stand still, but *cycles* always change and move. Wheels and rings effect a reconciliation between utterly opposite concepts, contradictions in terms: circular shapes express not only movement but also stillness.

Drawing a circle requires a pair of compasses, with each arm equally important to the operation, even though the point of one arm remains in one spot while the point of the other sweeps round the circle's edge. The central point of the circle, always equidistant from the line, is essential to the course of that line; centre and line in a circle embody, simultaneously, both difference and interconnectedness. The dot in the middle can be taken to mean stillness; the circumference or periphery (literally "the carrying around," in Latin and in Greek, respectively) then expresses movement, the other pole from the stationary.

Furthermore, the circumference of a completed circle, or indeed any closed outline, has no beginning and no end; it is endless, the Latin-derived word for which is "infinite." In a circle, beginning and end are one, wrote Heraclitus.[19] The endlessness of a periphery is of course very different from infinity viewed as a line extending without an end in space, or as time continuing lineally and forever. A circle can express either the notion of fullness and eternity or that of confinement and endlessness. The first pair (fullness and eternity) can represent heaven and the other (confinement and endlessness) hell. At a further level of abstraction, a circle expresses the mysterious coincidence of being and becoming (the first stationary, the second moving). A circle also reconciles two opposing spatial ideas: that of area and that of line, two dimensions and one. Pictures can be good for reconciling opposition for us: they put together what we have — often painstakingly — learned to see as separate. A picture is there to be turned to when we want to see things whole. But as I said, each time we do this, we have to be careful.

Diagrams can also be useful for thinking our way out of social and moral dilemmas, for helping us to look at things differently — or, alternatively, for ensuring that we keep on thinking the same thing. For example, we commonly use pictures in our minds of lines, limits, and boundaries when we are categorizing or creating order in the flux of our experience. Ideas are grouped and then set apart from each other, in order to clarify differences. This is an entirely necessary procedure, though full of traps and occasions for error. Human beings too can be categorized in groups separated by boundaries: the metaphor is that of frontiers, borders, fences, and their policing. This can lead, if no conscious moral principles transcend the categorizing, to racism and other forms of ranking people according to arbitrary criteria. To this subject we shall return.

The trouble with seeing one's life as a journey (a line), or one's self as an area bounded by a line, is that the image is essentially flat. The English expression "to be in a rut" is a linear one, and a series of recurring, unavoidable, unwanted consequences we call a "vicious circle." But ruts and vicious circles are escaped by getting out of them; we can change the image to one of rising to a totally different level. Conflicts can be resolved, as Hegel put it, not by killing off one or the other side, but through a new configuration: thesis and antithesis may be integrated and transcended by means of synthesis. The image of a spiral, for example, is that of a circle taking off into another dimension. The underlying diagrammatic metaphor is kept, but changed because of the movement's new direction — upwards.

The idea of a circle, on the other hand, even a moving one, can express time as eternally coming round to the beginning, to start again and repeat the cycle, just as the year repeats its seasons in always the same sequence. But because a circle is a closed form, because of its association with fate, and because of its flatness, it can also express human despair: no way out, no possibility of change, of breaking out of a fatal concatenation of events. ("Concatenation" is from the Latin *catena*, a chain: it suggests not only links tethering events, each one to the one before and the one after, but also a rope made from those links, binding a person against his or her will.)

An important aspect of the Christian revolution was a new resolve to break out of the ancient Greek and Roman view that human beings are in thrall to fate. Christianity's roots in Judaism provided it with a perennially powerful story about hope and freedom: that of the Exodus, or Way Out. The picture is of a journey of a people out of bondage to liberation. The journey took time, forty years — the number forty being a Jewish symbol for enough time, "the time it takes." This epic of liberation from captivity — through vision, determination, trust, and agreement to obey God's law — is a radical alternative to fatalistic thinking, to believing that the way things are is necessarily how they must continue to be. The biblical account of the Exodus made linear time, rather than cyclical time, a foundational metaphor for the West, and hence for any society influenced by the cultures of the West. Implicit in it is the concept of progress: human beings are able to free themselves, to learn, to achieve enlightenment. The road metaphor is kept but its meaning changed.

The English word "fate" is from Latin *fatum*, which means a thing said. All events were laid out (a spatial metaphor) in advance, written in a book of fate (writing, too, is lines in space), spoken, and hence fixed before ever the events occurred. A curse is a *fatum*: a thing said that must inevitably come to pass; a curse is a matter of time, not space. An implacable spoken or written law seems like fate to the person who must adhere to it; breaking such a law, once law courts and judges have been provided by a human society, leads to a trial. The word "trial" literally means a sifting out, here of those who obeyed from those who didn't. Later the word came to mean a painful test, because of the frequency of punishment for failure. Similarly, the verb "to doom" meant originally to pronounce judgement, but it ended up signifying consignment to an evil fate. "Doom" now means fate: not judgement in the end (as in "doomsday," an ancient word for the Last Judgement) but an ineluctable — and unwished-for — event.[20]

The hopelessness implicit in a belief in doom is overcome through looking not only ahead but also upwards — that is, above the diagram. One way of expressing this is to say that fate is changed thereby into destiny. The word "destiny" is from the Latin *destinare*, to make something firm, which itself comes from *stare*, to stand. A fixed destiny, an end or aim that is eventually reached, becomes the end or goal of a journey and a road: a destination. Destiny, in religious terms, is not confinement but fulfilment — in the unmediated enjoyment of a transcendent God (that is, a God who is above, or utterly outside and other than, anything like the metaphor of a fatal diagram).

Destiny is different from fate. *Fatum*, the foretelling, lies invariably at the beginning of our life's span. It also covers every twist and turn of our life's journey to its end, death, the most fatal moment of all. Where a circle is used as a metaphor for fate, time either is left out of the picture or becomes cyclic; fate is an outline in the sense of a strangling bond or an imprisoning wall. A ring can mean a promise freely entered into, like a wedding ring: promises commit people and are therefore binding. But a ring symbolizing encirclement by force is an embodiment of fate, a thing of power and oppression, like the Ring of the Niebelung, which curses whoever owns it. The One Ring in Tolkien's saga is always associated with fate as imprisonment: a perilous journey, twisting but linear, needs to be undertaken to undo its power, to release the world from the Ring of Doom.

Destiny, on the other hand, as destination, is the final outcome. It can also mean the line of life, but it always tends to remember and stress the end. Here, however, end means aim, what we strive for; it is not merely finality, the act of dying. Destiny therefore includes striving, intentionality, our own will. The object now is to convert the will (to "convert" is to turn over, to change and redirect) so that it aims not at something on the flat plane, which is all that fate or cyclic and natural determinism allows, but at something beyond fate, something we call "higher," or "the transcendent."

A Christian church is an example of a spatial metaphor for a person whose life is filled with desire to turn towards God, to rise towards a transcendent goal or destiny. This is a destiny offered to all, but on condition that each *wants* to reach it. Freedom here means looking first for the truth and accepting nothing that is found to be untrue. It also means deciding — wishing — to follow the truth, no matter what it takes to do so. This is part of the meaning of the Gospel declaration "The truth shall make you free."[21] A built church is a designed metaphor for this choice — the front door represents the choice — and this trajectory. Through its geometry, it represents an invitation to each individual visitor freely to respond to it. A church always respectfully insists that it is a metaphor. The person is the point, a person who is never thought of as merely part of a pattern.

A church is often built in the shape of a human body, and most transcendently Christ's body: the nave is the torso, the choir the head, the transepts the arms. It is also a three-dimensional metaphor for the "body" of people who believe in a destiny. Each one of them has a different life journey, but each — once the decision has been freely taken to join the group on "the way" — is also a brick or a stone, a piece of the structure. The metaphors express one of the great contradictions always inherent in living (though it is a contradiction that is a characteristically Western obsession because of our commitment to individualism, a commitment for which Christianity is in large part responsible): each of us is simultaneously an individual and a member of a group. Every individual person's journey is expressed in a church, as is the journey of everyone making for the single transcendent destiny that is God. The aim is in sight from the beginning, on entering the church. In many churches, the "end" is symbolized by the apse, where a depiction of "last things," or destiny, is typically to be seen high up, "above" the journey but still its goal.[22]

The fatal diagram, on the other hand, of a human being described as a flat area surrounded, created, defined by an outline, represents one individual alone, a wholeness, as self-sufficient as a ball bearing or the spherical earth moving through space. But a moment's reflection tells us that the earth is *not* self-sufficient; it depends on light and warmth from the sun, on being precisely where it is in relation to the sun in order for life to exist, and so on. And human beings are persons in fact because of other persons. They depend upon relationship, narrative, and meaning; upon culture and circumstances; upon communication.

The trouble is, other people detract from the freedom, defined as it tends to be in our culture as the self-sufficiency, of each person. They make demands, prevent or reduce possibilities, keep individuals "in their place." People live in groups of other people; their characters result from their own past lives, and their stories depend upon the lives and doings of people who are near them or who went before them. Living in society with others, while necessary for life and well-being, entails rules, otherwise uncontrollable violence will spread and society will break up and die out, taking with it the possibility of there being individuals to compose it anew. Freedom, socially speaking, is always compromised. There is a difference between what there is and what we want there to be. What there is is very often what we don't want. Freedom always, in one sense, involves a rejection; it always feels like an escape. What is broken out of is most commonly other people's power over us. Freedom requires protection from them, especially when those others feel free to try to change what is into what they want, and we find ourselves standing in their way.

That is what laws are for. They serve the ideal of freedom for each person in a society by providing conditions that everyone must observe: conditions for action, conditions for restraint. Laws are protective devices that underwrite the "line" around every individual. However,

lines or walls are different from what it is they enclose
and protect. Laws cannot make persons *want* to do anything, and above all, they cannot give persons anything to
want. They merely impose conditions upon actions. They
are negative rather than positive: they can prevent or punish abuses, but they cannot cause desires. Laws legislate;
they cannot create. Laws today are often called upon to go
beyond their duty. People too frequently have recourse
to the law when they are trying to resolve moral problems. They attempt to create and to state moral issues by
means of court decisions. But every time we think a
mere system can save us, we abrogate personal responsibility and let the metaphorical diagram take over. We
risk, ultimately, surrendering our freedom and settling
for fate.

A loss of personal responsibility, and therefore of freedom, also occurs where there is a refusal to address
causes when things begin to unravel — causes, after all,
have a disconcerting tendency to lie within ourselves and
our own behaviour. Not wanting to consider the causes
that are rooted in ourselves leads us to blame, then to
revenge and its soulmate, fatalism, a subject I shall discuss in the chapters to come. Every time we make a mess
of things, we think we can fix them by means of technology. This usually means concentrating again on
consequences rather than on causes. Instead of looking
honestly at ourselves, at the moral reasons for our failures, we look to science, whose prestige has become
overwhelming, to solve the problem: science in general
and technoscience in particular. The products of techno-

science are visible, after all — they are impressive; they *work*. A "smart bomb" may spectacularly destroy a target while the causes of the conflict remain unaddressed.

The primacy of science over culture, and all that culture implies of social, political, and moral activity, now seems indisputable. By the end of the twentieth century, we felt we had tried everything "culture" had to offer, from neo-pagan Nazism to Communism or materialistic collectivism. Many of us ended up wanting *no more groups*. We're understandably afraid of them, having suffered the ravages that groups enthralled by ideologies can inflict. Culture, which includes social agreements regarding belief, emotion, and enactment, has been accused of having failed; we are invited to "see through" it.

There are many cultures, we are constantly reminded — the word "culture" only recently has become plural — but only one science. Human cultures are all, we insist, of equal stature; it is easy, given the massive prestige of science, to slip into thinking that cultures are all equal because equally fictitious. Science becomes not only one but also the one and only bearer of truth. We forget that we ourselves are the very bricks and mortar of culture, which is nothing less than the way we behave and the expression of what we prefer to live by. Science does not, and cannot, prefer. We can, and do, because we are persons, not systems. And not only do we all have preferences, but there are reasons — truthful reasons — for preferring some kinds of behaviour over others.

The laws that human beings themselves have made may protect us, but they cannot make us who we are or what we want to be. Physical science is not going to help us either: technology can give us things to use, but it cannot provide us with purposes. We are forced to create culture for ourselves, just because we exist and are not alone. Living together is never a simple matter, but in the very fact that society is a human construct, not a "natural" one, there is hope. If society, morality, or culture deteriorates — if people are full of hate for each other, for example, or if we decide we've had enough of the ugliness and barbarity of our cities or the degradation of the environment — we can conceivably change the culture, because we collectively make it. Therein lies our freedom.

11

FATE AND THE FURIES

"IT WAS NIGHT IN SOME UNKNOWN PLACE, and I was making slow and painful headway against a mighty wind. Dense fog was flying along everywhere. I had my hands cupped around a tiny light which threatened to go out at any moment. Everything depended on my keeping this little light alive. Suddenly I had the feeling that something was coming up behind me. I looked back, and saw a gigantic black figure following me. But at the same moment I was conscious, in spite of my terror, that I must keep my little light going through night and wind, regardless of all dangers." When Carl Jung awoke from this dream, he realized at once that the figure was, in his words, "my own shadow on the swirling mists, brought into being by the little light I was carrying."[1]

Jung, an adolescent at the time, had for some while seen himself as split into two personalities. No. 1 was his ordinary, everyday self, and No. 2 was a "world of intuitive premonitions."[2] He interpreted his dream as

showing personality No. 1 bearing the light of consciousness and No. 2 following him like a shadow. "The storm
pushing against me was time," he wrote, "ceaselessly
flowing into the past, which just as ceaselessly dogs our
heels." He decided to go along with personality No. 1 in
his conscious life, and to separate himself for the time
being from No. 2. Later on, when Jung had found his
vocation and the road to his destiny was clear, the two
"streams" of his being flowed into one, and he became
what he said was a "united double nature": "It was as
though two rivers had united and in one grand torrent
were bearing me inexorably toward distant goals."[3] The
experience of watching himself enacting his dream, of
playing his other roles as dramatist, casting director,
director, and costume and set designer, and then the long,
conscious process of criticism and interpretation at last
helped Jung to see his destiny. Indeed the images with
which Jung *consciously* expresses his dream — the "river"
of time, with two tributaries that join together (this is the
"crossroads" metaphor, where one "road" splits into two,
in reverse), and the terror of time simultaneously "bearing us along" and "dogging our heels" — are some of the
most conventional images of fate and destiny.

Every human being is a born dramaturge, if only
because of the universal human habit of dreaming.
Nightly, in our dreams, we create structures intricately
patterned, rich with fantasy, and peopled with vivid characters who embody emotional intensity, meaning, and
design. Not only do we contrive and conjure up our own
dramatic creations, but we act in them as well, suffering

and discovering through the vicissitudes of the story. We are, at the same time, the audience at the spectacle: as our own dreams unfold, we watch and listen, spellbound.

B. S. —

We don't control events in a dream — although it is possible to learn, with careful effort and training, to change some of the things that make us acutely and repeatedly unhappy in our dreams. And even then, any tinkering we effect, any adjustments we make, must be extremely specific and limited. For the most part, we experience dreams as astonishing and filled with mysterious juxtapositions, unexpected information, and ineluctable direction: in that we feel powerless to change the outcome of our dreams, they predispose us to believe in fate. Finally, on awakening from our own dreams, we are left with the critic's role, that of interpretation. Dreams are full of meaning for us. Human beings are by nature — for example, in our dreams, which occur whether we want them to or not — committed to meaning.

Jung's dream is easily imagined by any one of us. We can see it as we read, feel the anxiety of it. The little light, the pursuing fiend, the wild dark setting are the stuff of thousands of myths and legends — the dreams that groups of people know through dreaming them together, awake and with deliberate art. Jung never forgot these elements of his dream, and his manner of retelling it, his naming of the shadow and of individuation through befriending the shadow, became a twentieth-century myth in its own right.

A story consciously told always keeps one foot in the world of dreams. It draws upon the universal experience of dreaming, and it shares with dreams the sense that sequence and intention, setting and style all issue from a source — the author's mind and psyche — that is mostly impenetrable to us. All we have to go on is what happens in the story and what is described — what is given. On this level, we who are not making up the story have simply no say. We submit to the author's vision just as we attend to the dreams that pour forth from urgent and creative forces in our own souls. Through metaphor and imagination, however, we are invited to work with the author, "going along with" her or his creation.

The reaction of the audience — and an audience's role is primarily to react — is, indeed, an indispensable portion of the story itself. The author writes to elicit the response, and in this sense, before the story even starts, the anticipated reaction exists; it continues after the author ceases the song. For the audience is like the dreaming self, attending to the story and the characters. It has no say, yet it gives rise not only to what is said but to the language and the images in which the narrative is expressed. The audience contains the story and the author; the author holds the story and the audience; the story constrains its author and its hearers. None of the three components is ever free from the other two. Narrative fiction is a binding and a patterning; a conspiracy is required for its telling. And a plot may be isolated and then named "fate." Believing in fate has probably always arisen in part because of the delights and terrors of storytelling. We have to realize — to learn — that in life we are not the readers but the authors of our own narratives.

In societies that are seriously committed to dreaming in common, stories become public property, and then even the author cannot change what is already known. The outlines of the plot — known already to everyone — must be accepted and inevitably provided when the tale is recounted, while the audience waits expectantly for what it knows must happen. Every parent who has read stories over and over again to a child knows how furious the listener can become if the least detail of the story is changed. Little *White* Riding Hood! The wolf without the anachronistic sleeping cap on! Inconceivable. The story may be elaborated — the contents of Little Red Riding Hood's basket might be negotiable or the woodcutter's clothes described if there is time — but the sequence of events and objects in the story that are nodes of meaning and springs for the imagination must be neither avoided nor changed. The audience demands them.

Different stories, different fates: the houses of the first two little pigs must crash in ruin; the statue of the Commendatore will certainly arrive on the doorstep to take up his invitation to dinner. Sometimes the constraints of pattern and of expectation become so concentrated that the plot itself produces objects and characters whose function is to govern the design, or actually to embody the inexorability of the tale as it unwinds (for a tale unwinds, like a rope or a thread). The wonderfully named Hope diamond dooms its owner inevitably to destruction: a thing of malevolent beauty, impervious to blame and incapable of pity, it attracts people into its orbit and proceeds to administer to them its curse, their fate. A story is like a web, with objects like the Hope diamond serving to gather up into knots and multi-layered intersections the energies of the story's momentum, creating the violent order and the patterned ferment that stories share with dreams.

When people create or enact stories, they project plot design into time and space. Imagination is embodied; dreams issue forth to become flesh. Sequence is always part of narration, for it is the nature of language to be spoken in time. But sequence, in a story, is beyond the control of characters and audience; it is a concatenation, or chain of events. We experience our dreams in space, of course, because that is how our senses perceive reality. (The dreams of the congenitally blind are no less vivid than those of the sighted: people are present, actions occur, and sensations are aroused like those of waking life.) In addition, our everyday language gives constant support to spatial readings of time. An expression like "of course" implies a course — a road or distance — that must be followed, a sense of being caught in a flow of events that takes on a momentum of its own. "By the way" introduces a subsidiary comment — something not on the route our words are taking. A group of actions is easily pictured as a web or a pattern in which we become implicated, which means literally "enfolded."

We may speak of actions as surrounded by circumstances (literally "things standing around" them) or in a context, a metaphor about time and space that derives from textiles: threads weaving lines into areas. Plot means not only a narrative but a piece of ground — a territory. It is almost impossible to speak without using a vocabulary that implies lines and areas, circles, roads, boundaries, bridges, and threads both spun and woven, creating designs with one dimension, or two, or three — and these for describing time, not space. Such habits of speech, like our habit of dreaming and our love of fiction, predispose us to accept — unthinkingly — a belief in fate.

Dreams are dreamed by each person individually. Stories, however, are consciously devised and then communicated. Stories demand interactions among characters. We ourselves live with others, who greatly influence — and help us to create — our identities. Knowing as we do that dreams and stories are time-patterned, and out of a need to use space to express contexts, relationships, and circumstances, we commonly extend the diagrammatic metaphor of area that we considered in the first chapter to include much more than the idea of one "individual" or outline enclosing its area. In ancient Greece the word for fate is *moira*, which derives from a verb meaning both to receive as one's portion and to be divided from. The portion is area, divided from other portions by lines. *Moros* in Greek means fate (like *moira*) or death. *Moros* is related to the Latin *mors*, death, and to "mortal," one who must die. Death occurs in a moment of time; death is an end of the rope of life, a cutting off, or a finishing line that we cross at the end of the course of a life. Death is a paradigm of fate: it will surely come, welcome or not. This fact can be blamed on no one, and it cannot be argued away; there is no reprieve. It is the metaphor of a rope or path or line that makes it possible for portion (area) and death (a moment or dot in time) to be linked in the same concept: fate.

The Greek word *moira* could also mean a piece of meat, cut from a whole roast served at a feast and given to one of the diners: it was this person's portion of the whole. Where a joint is carved up at the table, it has often mattered intensely both what piece a diner is given and whether he is served before or after the other guests. The piece represented one's rank within the group, how much one counted. A slice of pork or mutton, in such a context, could be inseparable from one's honour. Carving used to be referred to, in English, as "doing the honours."[4] And we still speak of one's "portion" in life, one's "slice of the pie." In these images, it is important to note, there is only a limited amount — of money, of jobs, of dinner, and then, when the diagram is used to describe social relations, of honour — to go around. The assumption is that the circumference of the "pie" sets a limit or boundary upon honour, just as the roasted pig is all there is for dinner.

Fatalistic thinking insists always upon the defining outline, upon "that's all there is." (A human lifetime, conscious as we are that it is limited in time, always reminds us that "that's all there is." A fence around a plot of land is a common embodiment of the idea of limit.) The Greeks called this outline *anangké*, which is often, and not entirely correctly, translated into English as "necessity." The word is rooted in the syllable *ang*, meaning something that squeezes. We have it in "str*ang*le," "*ang*uish," "*anx*ious," and even "*ang*le": angles are spaces pinched between lines. The container presses upon and constrains its contents; the rope binds the neck, the ring the finger. Fate sees to it that we carry out its decrees.

Fate as portion is also a picture of the extent of ourselves: what we might call our capacities (the English term is itself a spatial metaphor) or our identity. The Greeks preferred to speak of their *timé*, their honour. Where an honour system prevails,[5] the diagram tends to take on an overriding importance, expressing not only fate but relationship in society. Honour from other people — sanctioned by the opposite of honour, which is shame — both allows and circumscribes the portion or lot of one's life. Others decide how much room we shall be allowed in the diagram. Size is crucial — size that is relative to the "extent," or importance, of other people. Comparison is constantly made and competitiveness encouraged; negotiations are always ongoing, readjusting the importance allowed to each one by the others. Everybody is expected to try to be as "big" as possible — the area always pushes against the lines. All these attitudes are perfectly recognizable to us, since they exist in our own society also. But ideally, for us, they are regrettable attitudes, false ideals.

The diagram, I am sure you will have realized, has become a jigsaw of contiguous identities — although this jigsaw tends always to have pieces differing in size. Each area, surrounded by its line, is a part of the whole. It is jammed up against — indeed formed out of the lines surrounding — other pieces, other fates. Each area simultaneously represents the honour — the *amount* of honour — permitted to that human being. People are made to fit predesigned categories, and they must be inserted into those categories. Even if a person should fully concur with the category occupied, it remains true that the space has been provided, its size and position predetermined, by others. Honour is won by means of acceptance — and risks being withheld if there should be an attempt at escape. Honour and *moira*, pictured as geometrical designs in space, are co-extensive; any culture that is deeply invested in honour and shame tends always to believe strongly in fate.

Honour is always assigned by other people; a person is honourable insofar as he or she is honoured. The obverse of this is shame, and shame, too, is given or imputed by others. I must stress at once that I am using the word "shame" in a strict sense here, for we often say "shame" when we mean "guilt." The difference will become clear as I explain these concepts further. "Shame on you!" is a surviving English expression where the word is used strictly, because it is spoken by others to one of whom they disapprove. Shame is assigned by the opprobrium of others; a person, we often say, "is shamed" or "is covered with shame" (both passive voice). Shame is embodied in the rocks thrown at someone who is stoned to death for doing something shameful. Others throw these rocks at the wicked one; even the distance from which the stones are thrown is appropriately symbolic, because a shameful being is someone from whom righteous people want to stand apart in their outrage, even as they administer punishment. They want to make it clear that they themselves are different: faultless, therefore honourable. An ancient symbol of honour, on the other hand, was a crown, covering a person, this time in glory, encircling the head with a glorious *moira*. The crown, like honour, is — or should be — imposed by a person standing in for the rest of society. And a crown or a diadem, like a fate, is a binding thing.

This other-centredness of one's identity means that other people must be in a position, as we say, to judge and then to award amounts of honour or dishonour. Honour, therefore, demands display; other people are spectators and must be provided with a performance so that they can make their judgement. That is one reason why stories dealing with honour and shame love feast scenes and the presence of onlookers: the actors in the drama need an audience. Often a play will include an audience on stage, itself being watched by the playgoers. In ancient Greek drama, always saturated as it is with honour, shame, and fate, there was a chorus; it was as though an event occurring without onlookers was inconceivable — or simply not an event. The chorus of onlookers comment on the action: their reactions are indeed part of what is happening.

Honour arises from competition — it is always a matter of evident prowess — and is awarded by the people watching and deciding who has won. One person's honour is often increased at the expense of another's: what I take from you I add to myself, and by the same token, I must do everything in my power to prevent another taking from my stock of honour. Once again, it is as though there is a limited amount of honour to go around.

At the climax of the *Iliad*, Hector stands alone outside

the walls of Troy, facing the wrath of the unconquerable
Achilles. The Trojans crowd at the battlements, terrified
for the safety of their hero. (The watching crowd is essential for our understanding of the scene.) Hector's parents
beg him to retreat to safety behind the walls. But *moira*,
Homer tells us, literally "bound" Hector to remain outside
the walls.[6] The time has come for the life of Hector to end.
He is constrained not only by *moira* but also by his honour,
which here means his bravery and prowess in battle. He
cannot, he says, retreat before Achilles and so see his
honour diminished. Honour is never a question of common sense; it is, to an extent, the direct opposite of
common sense, for common sense is self-interested, cal-
culating, ordinary, and therefore small. His people are
watching: no, it is better to stay outside the walls, to fight
and die with honour.

The Olympian gods are also looking on. The goddess
Athene persuades Zeus not to intervene and save Hector,
his favourite. "Go ahead, save him," says Athene, "but
the other gods will not approve." Zeus could save Hector,
but Athene's argument is decisive: the other gods would
be outraged. (The gods too are bound by honour, which
is, as so often, co-extensive with and a version of *moira*.[7])
Zeus holds out his golden scales. The fates of Hector and
Achilles are weighed in the balance.[8] Hector's fate falls.
The great hero dies, with the prophecy on his lips that
Achilles is fated soon to die also — at the hands of the
coward Paris.

This tragic scene still reverberates with power for us,
and we can appreciate its nobility, the perfection of its

plotting, the selflessness and the bravery of Hector, even though its context is a society very different from our own. That difference arises partly, of course, from the epic genre in which the *Iliad* was composed. The fatal elements are there in part because the audience knew the plot in advance. Hector had to die at the hand of Achilles: that was the story! But the motivations, depicted as the binding forces of honour and fate, powerful and moving though they remain in the lofty context of the *Iliad*, are now out of bounds to us in ways we should keep in mind, even as we appreciate the magnificence of Homer, and even as we use a spatial and therefore quasi-fatal metaphor like "out of bounds" in this context.

The civilizations of the West have striven hard and consciously for two thousand years and more to liberate themselves from the thrall of honour and shame — those two, for honour and shame go together; they are two sides of the same coin. And together with honour and shame always goes fate, the relentless "given." Our Christian heritage has replaced — *ideally* replaced — the notion that a person is what he or she is in the eyes of other people. That true importance could conceivably mean size, or magnificence in the eyes of others. That there is something quasi-physical and therefore fated — an amount, a bodily factor, a percentage of a whole — about human worth. That we are what we do. That people's identities ought to be categorized, classed, judged by other human beings. That a person's role and social definition — his or her race or rank — come first; in other words, that some people can do anything because of who they are, and others are wrong whatever they do. That a wronged person is reduced in size and must therefore seek revenge to retrieve the amount of honour lost. That a person can be turned by an event into spoiled goods — as when a raped woman, having been shamed, must remain forever disqualified from marriage, even if what happened to her was not her fault. (It should be noted that shame culture is always heavily weighted towards power for males.) That what happens is fated, and hoping and striving for change is a waste of time.

Some of our most basic ideals consist precisely in turning down these beliefs and behavioural options. I do not mean that we always succeed, but that these are attitudes, rooted in honour and shame and once thought acceptable, self-evident, and even virtuous, that we try hard to discourage in ourselves. We are indeed guilty often of thinking in these ways, but when we do so we are betraying, not living up to, our ideals. We accepted in their place a moral system where guilt and forgiveness are supposed to replace honour and shame; where guilt is not merely the breaking of a rule but also remorse for having done so; and where guilt, if it is sincerely felt, can be effaced by forgiveness. Nowadays, honour and shame are allowed to infiltrate our values more and more, and with them seeps back a belief in fate, with its concomitant hopelessness. Two of the reasons for this are a falling away from Christianity as a moral source for the West, and a failure to understand how much we stand to lose thereby. For some perspective upon this large question, we need to look more closely at how honour and shame work.

When a person has been shamed, honour has been lost. It must be regained or the person remains reduced, dishonoured, his or her worth in the eyes of the community ruined. Shame cannot be forgiven: honour can be retrieved only by means of revenge. Part of that revenge will almost invariably include the publicity of the riposte: since others give honour to a person, they should also see the vengeance taken; they are watching. Guilt does not depend on other people knowing what you have done wrong. It always presupposes conscious voluntariness in the sinner. Dishonour, on the other hand, can be imputed simply because something unfortunate is seen to have occurred or an inadequacy revealed; moral fault might be, but is not necessarily, a reason for contempt. A cripple might be laughed at, for example, or a rich criminal's company found preferable to that of somebody innocent but ugly or smelly: a moment's thoughtlessness can precipitate anyone into shaming reactions. People in our own culture nowadays often complain that they are supposed to feel guilty for what they have done wrong. But guilt, though painful, is much less crushing than shame. And the most important thing about it is that it can be forgiven. Shame cannot be separated from the person's essence, whereas guilt can.

The much-maligned word "sin" refers to guilt and forgiveness, as opposed to shame and vengeance. In recognizing wrongdoing as sin, we do not lessen its enormity, but we do deprive it of its fatality. One is not guilty, to begin with, if one has not intended to do anything wrong. (In societies where ritual pollution rules, a person can be accounted "unclean" because of even accidental contact with something or somebody polluted. For example, the family members of a murderer may be shunned or castigated just for living in the murderer's house, whether they knew about his crime or not. Physical or familial proximity, not moral fault, is the point.) After the admission to oneself of guilt — one's own guilt, not another's — forgiveness can be sought. It is possible for a sinner to change — to express regret, accept punishment, make reparations. Forgiveness and guilt replace honour and shame in the name of the possibility of change — change in the guilty person, but also freedom from resentment in the person who has been offended, provided that the wronged person can accept a change and let go of resentment. Guilt and forgiveness together constitute a rejection of vicious circles, obligatory feuds, ritual pollution, inherited curses, and the ineluctable or otherwise self-evident need for revenge. Their aim is to liberate human beings from fate.

Forgiveness is provided by the person wronged; it cannot be demanded or forced from that person but is a gift, as the word "forgiveness" implies. Pardon, too, includes the freedom inherent in giving; the word is from *donare*, to give. To forgive is not, therefore, to lose anything. It is, however, to forego revenge. In an honour system, forgiveness therefore appears feeble; you have shown yourself to be merely too weak to fight back. As a consequence, you look small in the eyes of others — others being the whole point, remember — and small means not honourable. (In an honour system, being demeaned, despised, or made to look ridiculous — literally "laugh-able and therefore small" — is an especially painful form of shame.) In a guilt-and-forgiveness system, however, to forgive is not to show weakness at all: it is always an exquisitely difficult achievement. People can, indeed, use a false forgiving as a power ploy, to reduce the person said to be forgiven. Since belittlement is the aim, this is in fact a shame mechanism masquerading as pardon. Forgiveness, in a guilt-and-forgiveness system, offers freedom. It is a heroic ideal, not to be expected but always aspired to.

In any belief system related to Christianity, a person who feels guilt must learn to *accept* forgiveness, if not from the person wronged (from whom forgiveness can never be demanded), then at least from God, who is believed to be ready to forgive anyone who truthfully repents. To hang on to one's fault once it has been revealed, forgiven, and amends for it made — to refuse to move on — is to fall into shame, the opposite of guilt and forgiveness. For it means believing that one's very self has been diminished (a rejection of the idea that God loves and forgives), and it causes a subsequent descent into hopelessness. This is what people often call guilt. It is shame really, and fatal-ism, and they are right to think it a horrible thing. Calling it guilt can be a disastrous error if it leads people to think that the very idea of feeling guilty is evil.

To repent of the damage one has done, of course, requires humility — another concept that we tend nowa-days carelessly to reject. We confuse the feeling of shame — the misery of being diminished — with the lowliness or smallness inherent in the word "humble." But real humility is an aspect of honesty, of wisdom, of "the truth that will make you free"; it is also a direct challenge to the honour system's ideal that one should appear big in the eyes of others. Heroes and heroines, in Christian terms, are expected to be unassuming, to be aware of their short-comings, to see themselves in perspective, to avoid inflating their own importance or trying to reduce other people in order to enlarge themselves. Christian saints like Francis of Assisi or John of the Cross turn the honour system on its head by insisting always that they are not big but small. Having recognized their humility as truly a virtue, *we* decide that they are in fact great and admire them for it. We shall see that heroism is always rooted in other people's opinion, and therefore in honour and shame, but that it can transcend that fatal system.

Guilt and forgiveness depend upon a previous commit-ment, in a society that is making the heroic attempt to prefer them, to individualism. It's easy to see why. Wicked-ness can exist entirely in somebody's mind, unknown to anyone else, because guilt and forgiveness depend upon the interiorization of moral ideals, and upon the responsi-bility of each person for him- or herself. Pardon, unlike shame or revenge, cannot be demanded or imposed by other people; only an individual can forgive.[9] A totally different attitude towards size has come about: one that amounts to a redefinition of what constitutes importance. (It follows that whenever we claim importance for some-thing merely because it is big, we should think carefully about what we are saying.)

It is entirely possible, as our own history shows, for an

individualistic society to espouse honour and shame rather than forgiveness and guilt, so modern individualism will not in itself save us from fatalism. An honour system has often predominated, in at least some circles, in the nominally Christian civilizations of the West, and it has never ceased to survive or recur within our societies as a subset: in mafias, vendettas, or whenever people gear up for war. Honour and shame are always waiting in the wings; they can erupt anywhere, at any time. There need not be anything obviously reprehensible about such an eruption; it might even seem vivid and amusing — although not to the person reduced or shamed. For example, in Barcelona today a creditor can engage a collection agency that specializes in the haunting, in public, of a debtor: the one owing money is followed about everywhere he goes by a man in a top hat and tails. The tall, powerful stranger (he has to be prepared to defend himself if his quarry loses his temper) never needs to say a word. This picturesque ploy depends entirely on shame, on the fact that every Barcelonan looking on understands that the man in the frock coat is a walking embodiment of a sum of money owed and the fury of the person waiting to be paid.

Certain shame reactions that persist among us are worth maintaining — provided they are still useful, and provided above all that we see them clearly for what they are. They survive, for example, in codes of manners, and especially when we feel outraged by somebody breaking the rules of etiquette. The sociologist Norbert Elias has described how, in the course of the past four centuries in the culture of the West, what he calls "walls of shame" have grown up (notice at once the underlying presence of our diagram), separating each of us from all others.[10] He is talking of the small but vital signs and rules that are manners and politeness. "Don't spit"; "Never put your knife in your mouth"; "Don't pull faces" — and so on. Polite adults keep these rules — artificial as they are — almost automatically because they were taught as children to do so. Others in whom these rules were similarly inculcated demand compliance; they laugh at infractions or shrink in revulsion from anyone committing them. Somebody who chews loudly and with an open mouth — who has never been taught to eat correctly — will probably never be invited to dinner again, not at least by hosts who are proud of being proper and disinclined to make allowances. From such a sentence there is likely to be no appeal, for this is shame and shaming, not guilt. Manners, diagrammatically speaking, are lines merely. They are useful restraining and lubricating devices, but they should never be thought to be more. They present a moral façade but cannot count as morality, precisely because they depend on shame, not guilt. Wicked people, as we are all well aware, are capable of being extremely polite.[11]

Many aspects of honour systems are attractive. They keep people not only close but focused, alert, extroverted, and socially adept. They demand drama. We may certainly remain appreciative of their strengths, and even occasionally borrow them (knowing exactly what we are doing and why) where they are useful. Honour systems, such as that of ancient Greece, often go along with superb art and high culture. Courage is provoked and openly rewarded; self-esteem — where humiliation has not been allowed permanently to destroy a life — is honed and cultivated. And revenge is always easier than forgiveness, so satisfying, so ego-enhancing, so dramatic, so *natural*.

An honour system is communal, close, warm — even fiery. It insists on selfless loyalty to all those defined as being one's own. Individualism, on the other hand, can often feel cold and lonely. It seems at times to undermine every attempt at community. In an individualistic society, the very same diagram as that of the jigsaw we referred to earlier lies behind many metaphors for social patterning. Only here what is being said by the diagram tends to be that each area, each life, is complete in itself, separated from all the others, responsible for itself. Impingement upon others is discouraged, and the invasion of one's own privacy is experienced as an outrage. The image is like the one we looked at earlier, of a table set for dinner. Or a demand that others — especially strangers, of course — should not nudge or pat me too often, or stand too close while speaking to me, or sit down right next to me when I was hoping to be all alone on the beach. Individualism tends not only to protect but to isolate; it can trap people behind the walls that separate each person from every other.

What individualism demands — just as the whole point of guilt is the possibility of forgiveness that it offers — is for people to feel safe enough, ready and willing and free enough, to open up those protective barriers in order to notice, take care of, and finally love other people, even those not felt to be immediately rewarding or appealing. The outstanding characteristic of Christianity is its placing the highest value of all on love,[12] not only for one's family or group, but for everyone — including people who do things like chew with their mouths open. This insistence that love is greater than all the other virtues was, in the context of classical culture at the time of Christianity's beginnings, a revolutionary notion, since it appeared to downplay bravery, loyalty, honesty, obedience, dignity, and all the other ideals of ancient Rome. One of the social or structural reasons for the Christian insistence on love was the immense push that the new religion simultaneously gave to individualism. Without the transcendence love provides, individualism becomes a prison. Individualism requires transcendence so that the "walls," so wisely and carefully raised in order to shelter the individual from incursions by others, can remain — but be surmountable, for higher ends.

Without any conscious ideals held and understood in common, without intimate involvement with one another (whether because we are so busy, because we live so privately, because in public we are anonymous, because we need no one, have so little time, can't be bothered), without a creed we intensely believe in and are prepared to work and suffer for, with little faith that transcendence exists, let alone that it is possible — well, it is easy to begin feeling that guilt and forgiveness, let alone love for people not our kin or otherwise our own, are too difficult, not worth the effort. The alternative is ready to hand: honour, shame, and a consequent decline into fatalistic thinking. The slippage is first apparent in little things. Take for example the modern obsession with image.

It seems harmless enough — longing to make a good impression, to cut a figure, to look good. There's nothing wrong with that, surely? But if image becomes all there is, or even too large a part of what there is — if a person hides behind a façade — then something is wrong, given the still-existing presuppositions we live by. We may try desperately, therefore, having invested far too much in our look, to claw back some of the authenticity our culture demands of us.[13] It's not enough to dress well or wear the right makeup: our bodies must actually be beautiful, no matter what the cost in money and effort — thin, with perfect skin, rippling muscles, shining hair, and so forth. No wigs and corsets or even hats for us: we have to try to be — and to disclose ourselves as — the genuine article.

For image as pure façade is foreign to the ideals of our culture, and indulging in it or judging others by it — by the cars they drive, for example, the blocks they live on, or the brand names on their watches — leads us quickly into other attitudes that are equally alien. Honour is always loaded with physical proofs of itself. Externals are inevitable, for others must judge you and define you, so you must give them signs to judge by. An image can be just that: an external sign of what we want others to think is the case — even if it isn't. Our consumer culture itself makes the acceptance of mere image all too easy. "You are what you do" translates into "You are what you buy." To fall into the trap of identifying oneself with an object or an appearance is to flirt with fatalistic thinking.

In Greek mythology, the connection between fate and
timé — honour — was vividly brought to life in the
Furies. These were terrifying mythological fiends who
inhabited the "lines" of the diagram, both of fate and of
honour. They saw to it that vengeance was carried out for
crimes that were thought of as not only shameful but also
polluting. The function of the Furies was to keep categories clear, which is to say unmixed, unpolluted. They
were not only upholders of honour and vengeance and
purity but also the handmaids of fate. Greek drama
speaks often of the Furies, and also brings them onstage.[14]
They were the Angry Ones: Erinyes, their Greek name,
was thought to come from an Arcadian word meaning "to
be furious." The Furies were female, with snaky hair and
bloody eyes, iron feet and snatching hands; there was
nothing abstract about their shapes or their behaviour.
(Jung's Shadow, we may recall, was also a black figure,
pounding after him, dogging his heels, as was the
Barcelona debt collector in his long black coat and top
hat.)

Family always invites thoughts of fate, and the family
was the special province of the Furies. Family means ties:
unconditional relationship, sexual prohibition, careful
classification. You may choose your spouse, but nothing
will make you other than the offspring of your father and
your mother. And siblings are not yours for the choosing,
either. In ancient Greek myth, one who killed a member
of his own family, whether he intended to do it or not
(moral responsibility was less important than the fact that
the unspeakable had been done), was hounded by a pack

of Furies, the Angry Ones, for having blood on his hands. When the Furies caught him, they surrounded him and tied him up, tangling him in nets and ropes, the "lines" of categories and boundaries, the web of fate. They sang over him a song of triumph, binding him in their spell. Then they sucked his blood and tossed away his withered body. He had to pay with his blood, since the spilling of blood — the blood of his own! — had been his crime.

People today often lament the breakdown of the family. They rightly claim that individualism, here, has gone too far. But we should not forget that one of our most powerful moral ideals is that of caring for people *not* of our family. We have struggled hard — with varying success — to break the fatal aspects of family ties and the implication of all of a family in the honour of each of its members. (A mafia calls itself family because it roots itself in honour, shame, and binding vendetta.) The modern failure of commitment within the family should be lamented not because it is "unnatural" (a crime against fate), but simply because it is a failure of love and responsibility. It is part of a social weakening that extends way beyond the family.

The myths of the Furies contain elements of what the modern philosopher René Girard[15] has shown to be the primordial myth and ritual of the scapegoat. Here a person is singled out to be blamed for a general breakdown of society into apparently uncontrollable violence. This person is heaped with opprobrium (in other words, shamed), accused of horrific crimes (typically of incest and kin murder, precisely the crimes that called up the

Furies), hounded out of the group, and then murdered (often stoned to death). Girard shows that all societies without exception were once guilty of this periodic rediscovery of unanimity through uniting against a chosen victim. The temptation remains: societies are often still guilty of creating scapegoats. The scapegoat mechanism, though dishonest, works for the self-righteous majority.

Girard shows how the Christian revolution, which, as we have seen, is largely responsible for the long and still-continuing struggle to substitute guilt and forgiveness for honour and shame, also revealed the lie at the heart of the mechanism of the scapegoat, the purpose of which was to rid a group of its own violence. "The truth shall make you free" means not only foregoing vengeance but also denying oneself the comfort of creating a victim and fastening the blame on that person for one's own wrongs. Acceptance of the truth carries a risk, however, for what shall we do with our violence if we do not succeed in renouncing it and lack a scapegoat mechanism to divert it?

At the end of Aeschylus' trilogy, *The Oresteia*, the cosmic conflicts expressed by the drama — between old and new, female and male, dark and light — reach a transcendent reconciliation. The answer turns out to be the establishment of a law court and trial by jury. From that point on, murdering somebody could begin to be thought of as breaking (we still use the word "breaking") a written rule, rather than piercing physical and categorical boundaries so that automatic pollution, in the shape of filthy and spreading disorder and confusion, would ensue. Understanding the usefulness of law as a way of transcending infectious, polluting consequences was a tremendous achievement. Yet ritual pollution continued to be a force in ancient Athens. The Furies remained a threat, should people break kinship taboos. And it was still required that any charge of murder be brought to court by a family member — one of the victim's own. In this way, the law bowed to the honour system; it allowed for revenge.

A modern law court continues to provide an impersonal standard: the law, devised and constantly watched over by society as a whole and not only by interested parties. Punishment is decided upon by the court and carried out by agencies separate from the persons who have actually suffered from the wrongdoing. A law court's intention is to substitute itself not only for moral and ritual pollution but also for laws of vengeance. It is therefore always a falling back when, in our day, we carelessly start thinking of the law as a vengeance mechanism. There are cases where society must protect itself from people who cannot change their criminal propensities, but these are rare. A judicial system where convicted people are degraded or physically mutilated; taught to think of their identity itself as criminal; not allowed to change, make reparations, and then return to society — or even where they are deliberately kept out of the consciousness of people outside the prison — is espousing shame culture or even creating versions of the exclusionary scapegoat mechanism. When a condemned criminal is put to death and the victim's family members are invited to watch the death penalty being carried out, we again have a blatant survival from shame culture.

Science, as I said in the last chapter, has come to seem to many of us the only thing left that we can trust or admire. Yet science cannot by itself lift us out of fatalistic thinking; in fact, modern scientists on occasion seem to find nothing better than fate as an explanation for existence. The physicist Paul Davies recently claimed for the laws of physics an everlasting verity, "logically prior" both to the universe they describe and to the existence of matter itself. "We have to assume," he writes, that these laws "have an abstract, timeless, eternal character."[16] There could not be a clearer claim that these laws are like a pattern laid down in advance, although this modern scientist adroitly sidesteps phrases such as "laid down" and "in advance." He avoids the implications of these phrases because they point to a transcendent origin and aim for the universe, and transcendence is as unfashionable in modern science as it is in modern social thought. It is often remarked that the cosmology of every age faithfully reflects the culture of the people who draw the picture.[17]

Now, calling the laws of physics timeless and eternal is to attribute divinity to them, although since they are abstract they are not intentional, and certainly goodness is not mentioned, so that one need not believe in God to believe in them. In and of themselves, they constitute a mighty plan that is, using the metaphor of a plan, essentially flat, lacking the vertical dimension that is transcendence.[18] Yet in social terms, this "vertical dimension" is where human beings use their imaginations, where they search for better models for human existence, where they struggle towards liberation. The laws of physics are iron laws. Shorn of a transcendent dimension, they become a version of what the Greeks called *moira*: pattern pure and simple, the imprisoning outline of the universe, policed, in our nightmares, by the Furies.[19]

Unless, unless ... perhaps there is another geometrical model that can let us off the hook, so we can escape that relentless plan that is the diagram of fate. The ancient Greeks themselves thought of an alternative picture of the way things are. It too survives in our day. It is if anything more popular, considered more useful to think with, than lines and circles and webs of interconnection. We'll look at this alternative model in the next chapter.

III

FREE FALL

WHEN AN EAGLE FINDS A TORTOISE, then swoops down and seizes the creature in its claws, it is presented with a problem: how to get at the meat inside the animal's armoured exterior. The bird will often use its advantage — flight — to rise high into the air, drop the tortoise onto a rock, and so break its shell. One day an eagle did just that — but it mistook a man's bald head for a rock. The tortoise fell, struck the man's pate, and the blow killed him. Was this a chance event, or was it fate?[1]

The story was an ancient Greek one, and the man was said to be none other than the playwright Aeschylus, who not only was bald but also wrote poetry that revelled in vivid and concrete images expressing fatality. It seemed deliciously appropriate that Aeschylus should have been felled by a fatal tortoise, plummeting from the talons of an eagle.[2] Agreement was apparently reached that this event was fate, not chance, the reason being that chance is causeless. And the man's death did have a cause: namely, the eagle's wish to crack open the shell of the tortoise.

But the event could easily have been considered a matter of chance. The eagle made a mistake, after all; the affair was an accident. And it was surely a coincidence that the man, whether he was Aeschylus or not, should happen to have presented his bald head at that very moment. An even more powerful suggestion that this was chance could have been derived from the man's skull having been struck by the falling tortoise. The word for chance in Greek is *tyché*, from a verb meaning to hit or strike. A widely accepted metaphor for chance has always been that of things — often many things — careering through space and unpredictably colliding.

The word "chance" in English comes from the Latin *cadere, casus*, to fall, fallen. "Befall" itself means to happen to. And "happen" is from "hap," an event resulting from neither design nor intent. We double up this meaning in the term "haphazard," "hazard" being from the Arabic, meaning a game played with dice. Games involving the falling and rolling of dice always invite chance into the proceedings. The root of *cadere*, to fall, appears in the word "ac*cid*ent," a falling against: accidents are often a matter of chance collisions. A coin*cid*ence again has the syllable *cid* in it, from *cadere*: two apparently unrelated facts or events "fall in with" each other. In Latin, *casus*, like our "case," could be simply an occurrence (literally a "running up against"). It might also be a downfall or a false step: tripping and falling, whether literally or metaphorically, are archetypal accidents.

Chance is blind, and when personified, it tends to be a

woman blindfolded. She is random, indifferent, without design — unless she is taken to be lucky. Then she has no blindfold because she is directing affairs, seeing to it that things turn out well. When people reach for metaphors to describe purely random chance, they think of shuffled playing cards, tumbling lottery drums, horses wildly and spontaneously changing directions as they freely run ("random" is from the French for an impetuous gallop), ball bearings rolling and knocking together, coins flipped, bullets that ricochet. Blind chance is found in the realm of movement, of fluctuation, of spinning, speeding, pelting objects. Plurality, a lot of moving things, is part of many metaphors for chance, and also for madness: swarms of insects and wildly flapping multitudes of birds are common metaphors for insanity.

Fate, which tends to be expressed either as lines or as spaces enclosed by lines, is often experienced as heavy and limiting; the fatal diagram is like a prison. It is only natural that people should grasp at chance as the great alternative to fate, chance as an escape. The word "chance," in English, means not only fortuitousness, the opposite of fate, but also opportunity. Geometrically speaking, chance occurs at the points where lines — accidentally — intersect. But chance is usually represented not by lines or by circles, but by dots. Where fate is imagined as a diagram made of lines (continuous, static, lasting), chance is points and dots (bouncing, moving, temporary). Chance, unlike fate, implies change — or the chance to change — and movement. It is an obvious preference in the climate of modernity. Rather a rain of freely tumbling dots than the constraint of lines!

It is almost impossible for us to imagine today the extent to which our own forebears lived closely together, "on top of one another" as we might put it. Take bedrooms, for instance. We discover with a shock that whole families used often to sleep together in one bed; people did without corridors in their houses, so you could expect somebody at any moment to stroll through your bedroom to get to his or her own sleeping quarters. The rich thought nothing of having a servant always sleeping in a corner of the bedroom. Modernity rejects all this choiceless togetherness and modern technology has helped us avoid it, so people today can scarcely imagine what life so thoroughly lived in common used to be like. We sleep in separate rooms, live and eat in separate quarters, move about behind the closed doors of metal vehicles. In big cities we form anonymous crowds, busy, hurried, ignoring as far as possible others doing the same. Our problems, therefore, are very different from those of our ancestors in that it now requires considerable effort even to meet other people, let alone get to know them closely.

In the past, people demanded predictability and formality in manners. One reason for this was that formality creates distance, and occasions for distance from others were desperately needed. Distance had to be consciously provided, and even fought for, with all the "culture" at one's command. Nowadays, however, although technology has enabled us to revel in privacy or to connect at will electronically, we often find ourselves seeking for ways to gain sorely needed face-to-face access to other people, to say nothing of time spent in their company. We therefore choose, indeed demand, informality.[3] By carefully demonstrating informality — often an entirely ritual informality — we proclaim the important modern ideal of equality. But at the same time, informality enables us to break down walls of separation; it requires people to be, or at least to pretend to be, casual. Clothes should (apart from rare occasions) be unostentatious, comfortable, and everyday; address is usually familiar, manners simple.

The word "casual" again derives from the Latin *cadere*, to fall, that ubiquitous metaphor for chance (a "casualty," remember, is an accident). And manners as casual behaviour leave a good deal to chance: people are invited to "come as they are," to "sit anywhere," to "drop in." All this freedom is habitually associated in our minds with chance: chance as opportunity, as escape, as to do with openings rather than with closures. Human beings are as free and as self-sufficient as rolling stones — like dots, moving in space.

This image — again it is geometrical — was also common in ancient Greece, where it arose out of a desire to escape from a philosophical quandary. The Greek philosopher Parmenides had said that Being was One. He pictured this Oneness as a giant sphere, utterly full of Being. "Nothing" was expelled beyond its periphery. One and still was the truth, said Parmenides and his followers; the perception of variety, of Many and moving, was merely illusory. And the boundary of the sphere of Being bound the whole singular sphere in its grip; it was the outline we described earlier, the "fetter" of fate, *anangké*.

The greatest achievement of Parmenides — it turned out to be essential to the development of science — was his realization that our human senses do not give us access to all of the facts about the physical universe. Thought alone — he thought — might reach the truth that lay behind appearances.

The philosopher Democritus and his teacher Leucippus dedicated themselves to exploding Parmenides' picture of Being. That picture had amounted to a breaking apart of two of the ancient philosophical oppositions that were believed to constitute the universe: those between One and Many and between stillness and movement. Democritus was said to have had his flash of inspiration one day as he noticed particles of dust as they sank, glittering, in a sunbeam slanting through a window.[4] He saw them moving. What was it that permitted them to do so? It was the fact that each of them was surrounded by space! What if *movement* was real and *immobility* illusory? What if Many, and not One, was the fact — many tiny things, each solid and real, complete in itself? These many things would be far too tiny for us to see (Democritus followed Parmenides in accepting that our senses need not perceive what truly is), and they would be surrounded by the Empty. What is not, said Democritus in opposition to Parmenides, has being: "No-thing exists just as much as Thing."[5]

The One of Parmenides was indivisible. Democritus refused to believe that all was indivisible, any more than that movement was merely an illusion. Instead he proposed that plurality was the secret of matter, and that that explained its divisibility. All was made of particles and space, the particles endlessly moving. The concept of indivisibility remained, however, for there had to be a point, he reasoned, a tininess, at which you could divide no further. He made indivisibility a property of the particles rather than of the whole. He called his particles atoms, meaning "things that cannot be split." Lacking any instrument resembling a microscope, with no conception even of experimental science, let alone of particle physics, Democritus and the rest of the school that came to be known as the Atomists intuited the nature of matter to be in fact the agglomeration of invisible particles.

Democritus' atoms had shape, size, and nothing else but their position; taste, smell, and our other senses are conventions or illusions produced by colliding atoms.[6] Everything we see — and that includes ourselves — is atoms arranged in clumps. This massing, in his view, the atoms achieve entirely on their own, with neither guidance nor design. They simply fall because falling is their nature, and they sort themselves and clump themselves because it is their nature to do so: things that are similar tend to congregate.[7] The atoms are infinite in number, with geometrical extension, and immortal: the only change they undergo is that of position. (It will be noticed that atoms, like *moira*, are diagrammatical in nature, being made of nothing but shape, size, and position in space; they are therefore divorced from living realities such as human persons, although they can be thought to direct them, "be applied" to them, and even to represent them.) Democritus said that the atoms constitutive of the universe gradually form vortices in space and begin to spin as if in a whirlwind, or like water going down a plughole. One of these whirlpools of atoms we perceive as our world. Eventually the vortex will run out of energy; our world will disintegrate, setting the atoms free to fall again singly through space.

But for Democritus, none of this happens by chance: "Nothing occurs at random," he said, "but everything occurs for a reason and by necessity."[8] Democritus' view was that what appears to be chance (the collision and ricochet of atoms) is unpredictable only because we do not know all the facts. If we could encompass in our minds the speed, shape, and size of each of the myriads of atoms, and the preceding concatenations of events propelling each of them, we would know why everything happens and be able to predict it precisely. This we now call determinism, the "billiard ball" approach to cause and effect: everything is blind, certainly, but everything is predetermined, ineluctable, automatic. This brilliant alternative to the ancient diagram of fate, however, not only made a mockery of free will but also negated meaning.

It became fashionable in the late twentieth century for intellectuals apparently to despise meaning — and certainly to flee from it. There has been a death of the self, it is said; in terms of *moira*, any outline that might surround us and give us a shape has been rubbed out. Meaning involves connections that are not merely chance collisions. It implies some sort of system that "makes sense." This could well be a reprehensible or a mistaken system: it is thought better, therefore, to hold oneself apart from meanings, just in case. Some go further and claim that any system is invariably illusory, that anything that resembles a thought structure — a theory, a story, a sentence, even language itself — is made up, and therefore fictitious. We live inside our language, which is artificial and corresponds to nothing outside itself. We can make connections if we like — but we must realize that always we are merely playing with words.

This is a modern version of believing that chance is all there is. It is the latest sect of the ancient faith that the real is in fact an innumerable crowd of invisible, immortal, meaningless particles drifting through space. Our own modern heads (rather than our whole bodies, for we are talking here of intellectuals) are like Democritean atoms, the thoughts inside them hermetically sealed off from incursions from without and indisposed to venturing forth among what are reckoned to be mere phantoms. Having chosen this faith in preference to what they protest is a facile belief in meaning, its adherents often feel heroic about their lucidity and about the frustration they have chosen to impose upon themselves. They, at least, are honest. They are strong enough, and brave enough, to face the abyss: the random yet predetermined impact upon themselves of language and experience. Looked at from a different perspective, however, an apparently heroic acceptance of meaninglessness can be in fact an easy cop-out: it undermines, for people "sitting pretty," all constructive change and all of politics. The word "fortune" means not only chance but money. It is usually people lucky enough to be comfortably off who enjoy playing with the notion that all is chance.

Now, it is certainly true that merely studying the meanings of words or inspecting the rules of syntax will not lead one to understand the world. And I have already said that visual metaphors can be misleading. It does not follow, however, that we should use no metaphors, or that language is only a mirage. All of us use language — indeed, it is possible to show that the capacity for speech (which implies a reaching for meaning) is constitutive of our humanity. If everything evolved by chance, it is surely fair enough to ask why and how chance evolved in us a demand for meaning.

Modernity does its utmost to avoid both meaning itself and the implications of an apparently innate desire for it. Meanwhile, a painful lack of connectedness among persons results in our granting to time a role that is as unifying and constricting as are shame and fate in an honour/shame system. Clock time, which is our way of keeping as much of society as possible on one schedule, controls modern behaviour as nothing else does; it keeps people within bounds, through time experienced as both limited and a fatality. We use nowadays two kinds of clocks, one parcelling out time in space, the other dividing it into numbers and dots. In either case, "the time" on the dial or digital panel of a clock or watch becomes visible, a thing to be looked at. We are then expected to force ourselves to live according to it. Time as visible space or as number is inhuman, a version of fate, because it is separate from the way we actually experience our lives, and yet our lives are forced to conform to it.

Very early and intelligently, human beings learned to relate time to the voyage of heavenly bodies through space; many and ingenious are the ways subsequently devised for measuring time as lengths. "The time it takes to cook rice," in Madagascar, is synonymous with "The distance one walks in about half an hour"; expressions substituting time for space and space for time are common the world over.[9] Time can be expressed as volume — for example, as the amount of water that has taken a certain time to trickle through a hole[10] — or as a pile of sand (ground eggshells were found to be more accurate) running from one container in an hourglass or minute timer to another. Sundials still survive, marking time with stripes of shadow cast by the sun and moving over areas of measured-out space; at night, when there is no sun, candles were sometimes used instead, their sides marked at intervals that took a roughly predictable time to burn down. Ever since, because candles dwindle as time passes, they have poignantly suggested the fragility and brevity of spans of time — and especially of human lives, so quickly over, so easily snuffed out even before necessity must end them.

Clock time, divided into mathematically equal bits, is that of an hourglass endlessly emptying and being reversed. On a dial, we marshal the tumbling grains into a line, marching round and round in a circle, accompanied by tireless "hands." Such a circle we call a clock's "face," round like the horizon and like the sundial it replaces. Ticking clock gears or the tick-tock of a pendulum are also like heartbeats, which are readily imaginable as segments of a passing lifetime; when the beating stops, that life's span is at an end.[11] People have shown a remarkable fidelity and even affection for clock faces, in spite of the invention of the digital clock or watch, which has connotations that far more closely mirror what are apparently the defining characteristics of modern life. Perhaps we find circular watch and clock faces more human and therefore more attractive to us, more meaningful.

The digital clock or watch avoids portraying time as geometrical space. The shifting figures, the blinking dots, are as separate as falling grains of sand, counting hours and minutes past and marking the present instant. The number of minutes that have elapsed in each hour are shown, but we cannot "see" (as we can on the *moira*-related clock face), and therefore have to compute, how many minutes are to come. Digital clocks represent time as repetition, as a "powder of moments,"[12] every granular one of them exactly alike. Connection among these moments is a matter of adding them up. Representing them as numbers, however, goes on to provide for them an inescapable sequence, as binding as a chain.

Clock time — any clock time — fails to express the human experience of time lived — its *longueurs* when we are suffering, its speeding by either when we are pressured or when we are happily absorbed in meaningful activity. Numbers count, calculate, and compute, rather than link or suggest or characterize. Numbers properly understood are magnificent: many a cosmologist has asserted, since Pythagoras did so in the sixth century B.C., that the universe is made out of numbers. But numerical figures can also be experienced as unforgiving and alien, especially in a society such as our own, where numbers — even numbers of people — are often preferred to the people themselves. Numbers, like *moira*, point to persons only insofar as they fit a system. They therefore in fact leave persons out of account.

The modern science of statistics measures frequencies, discovers probabilities; it distinguishes between significant and merely random differences among frequencies. It is a brilliant means of dealing with — that is, discovering meaning in — non-systematic processes or apparently chance events. But the subject matter of this science is most pertinently ourselves, human beings, each of whom is unpredictable because capable of making choices. We are grateful for the en bloc predictions about group behaviour that statistics promise us. However, apart from the fact that there is something irritating about being questioned and counted and having our behaviour anticipated, our suspicions are aroused if we wonder about the methods by which information about us is collected. Are what these people call the samples of us really representative? Are the right questions being asked in order to reach a reasonable result? How much insight do the researchers possess into the issues they are supposed to be investigating? What are they counting us for? Who is seeking this information, and how will they use it?

Numbers are applied to us in many other ways as well. We live by clock time, and just because each of us is so independent of others and lives his or her life so separately, we have even been persuaded to strap little clocks onto our bodies in order to be synchronized with society at all times. We are counted by census; we vote — but also put up with pollsters who tell us how we are going to vote. We grade students' papers and make judgements such as "She's a C." We undergo IQ tests. It is often carelessly accepted as a fact that only what can be measured should count as a fact. (This belief itself, of course, cannot be measured.)

All of this docile reliance on numbers is undergone partly in order to reduce the domain of chance in our lives. Statistics permit prediction; they represent a great step forward in human understanding because they have introduced into modern thinking the liberating concept of probability — not necessity but *probability*. To this idea we shall return. On the other hand, however, numbers, and also frequencies, are utterly inhuman. It is demeaning, and intentionally so, to label somebody — a prisoner, for instance — as a mere numerical figure, and then to refer to him or her as that number. Quite apart from the errors that can be propagated by statistical science poorly performed, it is unavoidable that statistics should reify. "Reification" literally means the turning of an idea, an opinion — or a human being, in the case of the prisoner — into a thing. Pollsters and statistical researchers begin by collecting answers to questions they have devised. These scrappy, cramped replies are then mixed, counted, their frequencies measured. Our preferences and opinions are treated as objects; when enough of them are collected, they are turned into predictions about how huge numbers of people will behave. A person who gives an opinion becomes dissociated from that opinion. The opinion takes on an atom-like, qualificationless existence all its own; it goes on existing even should the now irrelevant person who gave it change his mind. Next comes the publication of the prediction — how we shall vote or what soap we prefer. And I learn that should I personally disagree with the conclusion, what I think means nothing whatever.

The answer being sought is not who or why but *how often*. (*What* is being investigated is decided in advance.) Now, a frequency might be a riveting piece of information for people selling soap, but it rarely means much to me. It is true that statistics, such as "7.7 per cent of wives hate their husbands," or "There are 5.2 per cent more delinquents this year than last," have become popular in sidebars in newspapers, magazines, Websites, and TV screens. We read them with a slightly numbed fascination — deluged with them as we are and feeling that we ought to be informed about these things — but we realize that we are powerless to change them, at least as they stand, triumphant in their little solid boxes on the page or screen. Numbers quickly turn into chains — concatenations, fatal bonds — complete with links, knots, and consequences, but in the end separate from ourselves, utterly beyond each person's capacity to alter them. Numbers drift past us or rain down upon us like the atoms of chance, indifferent, multitudinous, atomistic, impervious.

How often is not the only question adored by the culture we live in. There are also *how much* — both quantity and price — and *how fast*. It is important to recall that the really important questions — those posed mostly directly and profoundly by religion — are *who* and *why* and *how*. Democracy, which continues to be at least in theory our ideal, also requires us to ask such questions. *Why* and *how* and *who* are questions that point to transcendence, to rising above the fatal diagram and the no less fatal space or flux outside it. Not asking these questions leads us into the death first of religion, then of democracy, and finally of politics itself. What happens in the end is a descent into mindlessness, or at least into meaninglessness.

Facts themselves can become a matter merely of quantity — a meaningless, unconnected, unremitting jumble. The expression "brass tacks" is rhyming slang for "facts." It poetically expresses the inhuman hardness and piercing rigidity, the singleness and interchangeability of facts without links among them. It is a terrible thing to be bombarded by facts — even if they happen to be true. (They often, of course, also happen to be untrue.) Thinking — even the thinking of a postmodernist — is a patterned activity. A geometrical theorem includes a joining of points; what is created thereby is a diagram. The words "theorem" and "theory" both derive from the Greek word *theoreo*, meaning "I see," in the sense that "I contemplate, using my reason," and then "I understand." It is normally impossible to see, or to have insight, through a heap of random facts, all of them presented as having the same value. Indeed, it is usually necessary to limit the number of facts at the thinker's disposal, to decide which ones are relevant and discard the rest. That is why so much time must be spent when doing research, for instance on the Internet. Not merely getting the facts but finding the *relevant* facts is the indispensable beginning of thinking. We speak, for example, of a "framework" in which we think. This is a diagrammatical metaphor about lines and limits.

Understanding full well the problem with a deluge of information, the Internet always insists that it offers us connection and meaning. It does this by calling itself a "web" and a "net," using images of lines rather than dots. (The ancient Furies, handmaids of fate, were also said to catch their quarry in nets and webs.) We are offered what is called an information highway — a path, a fate-like path, through the mountains of debris. The information highway is in one sense a new version of bureaucracy, in that it collects, channels, and sorts information. But who does the collecting in the first place, who the sorting, and how are these achieved? Like bureaucracy, the abuse of which often turns into a metaphor of modern mindlessness, the Internet is supposed to serve us by ordering information, but it can easily lead us into a trap in which it makes important decisions on our behalf while relying on less than adequate knowledge, wastes everybody's time, and may even on occasion serve nobody but itself.

On another level down — for I am tracing a descent, a decline into meaninglessness — facts become merely trivial. Trivialization is, I believe, a deliberate social strategy in which facts are reduced to insignificance. First they are atomized, disconnected from anything like a system. The game called Trivial Pursuit, for example, plays with artificially isolated facts as though they were counters. What it requires in the adept, however, is a honed version of the universal human ability first to make one's own reasonable system of relationships, second to arrange aspects of one's experience in that system, and third to remember where the material was placed so as to retrieve it. The point is that memory itself is impossible where chance rules like a meaningless drift of atoms. Memory requires order and sense.

Trivialization is a process of belittlement. It flattens everything out, reducing it to one smallness. It takes over, however, by means of artifice; as I said, I believe that trivialization is often deliberately achieved. For example, important things can be placed in inappropriate contexts and so rendered ridiculous. Trivialization often refuses distinctions — between sacred and profane, say, or between public and private. There is a constant wearing down of links and connections, rendering them weak and pointless. Information — the evening news, for example — is provided in self-contained, unconnected sequences, with each event given a similar emphasis. A football goal may get the same amount of coverage as an earthquake, only a little later in the program. The advertisements, meanwhile, receive more care and the expenditure of more artistic talent than anything else on view. One effect of all this, of course, is apparently to leave one arbiter, and one only: the person confronted with the millions of flattened-out, trivial facts and reports on facts. Immediately we see how useful trivialization is in a consumer culture. For this person, this arbiter, finds that the only discriminating factor left is his or her own preference or desire (I nearly wrote "opinion," but at this stage thinking has become dormant).

To trivialize is thus to make each onlooker a little god — a very little god — free to choose his or her pleasure. It promises freedom. But first it has made freedom meaningless, since there is no longer any enduring point in choosing one small thing rather than another. No *enduring* point, because there is — there must be — a satisfaction of desire to be found at some particular moment, otherwise future desires will themselves become discouraged and, finally, die. A collision occurs, person meets object like the click of one billiard ball striking another. And then another stimulus and momentary satisfaction of a desire — a sexual contact, something to buy, another cigarette — must be sought. Not only reasons but consequences are routinely rejected as unimportant, irrelevant to the satisfactions of the present moment.

At a lower level still, meaninglessness feeds on ignorance. It is difficult to make for oneself a highway through swarms of colliding facts, to be able to distinguish between the important and the trivial. It is harder still to make decisions about what to prefer and how to act once the distinctions have been made. And it is impossible even to begin without basics: a firm foundation of knowledge and an understanding of why some things are preferable to others. (Basics or foundations are themselves linear concepts, enemies to chance as meaningless dots.) It is therefore not only foolish but also cruel for a society to deny to any of its citizens the best education it can provide.

Yet we refuse to educate. We do this because we are lazy. (It takes enormous effort and talent to teach people well — and it is also difficult to be a student, to accept the discipline required by learning. In any case, people have first to see the point of learning.) Sometimes we seem actually to believe that "de-skilling" the population is useful: people will be quiet because they are incapable. If they are ignorant, they might even buy more! We seem to think that no consequences will follow from our neglect. Indeed, we often fail to think about it at all.

Not bothering to think about it causes a further slide into meaninglessness. We are tired; we have no time. And here we return to the subject of clocks. The perception that we have no time is one of the distinctive marks of modern Western culture, a precondition of our social system as much as it is a result of it. No time is used as an excuse and also as a spur: it both goads and constrains us, much as honour and shame did for the ancient Greeks. Time, having been rendered scarce, remains abstract, quantitative, unconnected with ourselves as persons — as amoral and unarguable as fate. It exerts pressure on each person as an individual (each of us obediently wears that watch). The feeling that we have no time escapes explanation and censure through claims that it is a condition created entirely out of our good fortune. We have no time apparently because modern life offers so many pleasures, so many choices, that we cannot resist trying enough of them to use up all the time we have been allotted. We are induced — in this case by a battery of constant distractions — actually to enjoy having no time. It is, after all, the people considered the most important among us who seem to have the least time; there is enormous prestige attached to keeping a great many balls in the air at once. And keeping busy and distracted has the additional advantage of preventing us from thinking.

It's hard for a lot of people to see, these days, that it matters if one fails to keep appointments, breaks promises, or refuses to apologize because it's a nuisance. (Failing to apologize can be yet another sign of a fall back into honour and shame: an apology may seem like a relinquishing of part of one's honour.) All such minor lapses of consideration for others are the snippings of connections, the diminution of human relations themselves to the indifferent collisions of chance. For a while, the rule of chance feels like freedom because it involves an escape from fatal ties, from obligation. It doesn't take long, however, for lassitude to creep upon us, exhaustion from trying to cope with multitudinousness, busyness, and repetition without any sense, and this can finally lead to depression, a disease that has become an epidemic. Flatness, of course, results also in an all-pervasive boredom — and a compulsion to seek further distractions.

The eighteenth-century father of the free, or laissez-faire, economy, Adam Smith, dared to postulate an optimistic view of fate. If you left people alone to follow their bent in the field of economics, he assured us, the market itself would apply what he called an "invisible hand" to correct imbalances, to keep us on the tracks. (Railway lines, soon after their appearance, became and remained a favourite modern metaphor for fate.[13]) We still appear to think that we can rely on the market — quasi-personified like one of the Furies, complete with its "invisible hand" — to regulate the domain that economists have allotted to it, of scarcity or limited availability on the one hand and consumer demand on the other. The market (which, we need to remind ourselves from time to time, is us — the people actually doing the buying and selling) appears to operate independently of our own will, rather as, for Marx, "the logic of production" and "the march of history" existed as fatalities in their own right. It is like letting the spatial diagram of fate rule rather than serve us, or like refusing to leave the house and then feeling imprisoned. Whatever the reasons for the doors being shut and locked — whether it is our bottomless greed combined with limited natural resources (as the economists assure us is the case), or whether we have become convinced by a kind of ascetic rationalism that rationalism (what else?) rules everything — the result is the same: we feel it is useless to struggle. We are caught, helpless, in the webs and bonds of the Furies, of fate.

My point is that helplessness is as surely a result of chance as it is of fate. However, we need not imagine that everybody in our culture is helpless. Far from it. There are plenty of wily creatures about, and they are only too anxious to manipulate the boredom of others and their sense of futility. Take, for example, gambling, investment in which has grown enormously in recent years. Gambling fits modernity like a glove because it is about chance, fatalism, and meaninglessness. With a click, a bounce, or the number of dots on a die, it turns chance into fate. Gambling is a powerful distraction from boredom because it is both effortless and dangerous; it is a temporary escape from a mindless yet pressure-ridden reality. It is about money, about addictive repetition, and about immediacy: I collect my wad — or lose it — *now*. And then, in the rush of triumph or of increasingly desperate hope, I try again. Eventually the very rush becomes an addiction.

Our own governments permit, or even themselves erect, palaces in which people are invited to gamble. (The Internet, of course, increases the number of such offerings, and the easy response to them, immeasurably.) Our rulers then manage to feel self-righteous about it, claiming that gambling — that is, the profits that such set-ups invariably make — provide them and us with funds. We have learned to hate paying taxes, forgetting that justly distributed taxes are foundational for democracy. Having come to resent being asked to provide the funds for what we need, we are now invited to have fun gambling instead. It is true that civic responsibility is more difficult, more creative, and more human than the mindless rolling of dice. In any case, how can we expect people who feel helpless to be either far-sighted or unselfish enough to undertake the transcendent ideal that is democracy?

The stock exchange is itself a gambling casino.[14] The millions of facts, the "brass tacks," that are needed to know what the market will "do" next (as though the market were a creature and could do anything at all) are simply unavailable to the bettors and the gamesters within the brief window of time allotted for making decisions.[15]

Gambling on the stock exchange means guessing and submitting to chance. And here, where chance is king, chance is also the only form of justice there is. Knowing has nothing to do with chance, and therefore knowing something vital to the proceedings that the other players cannot know, and acting on it, is doubly unjust: it is like pretending to be fencing but using a real sword. Insider trading is common enough on the stock exchange. Many a gambling casino or slot machine in fact fixes the amount of money it can lose, so that its own profits are assured. "Invisible hands" have a tendency to belong neither to chance nor to fate. They would in fact be highly visible, if you only knew to whose arms they were attached.

Ours is not a permissive society, or at least not primarily a permissive society, as many claim. It is, rather, an addicted society. Permissiveness suggests freedom and escape, but — make no mistake — addiction is a binding, by an unbreakable attachment. We have devised all sorts of sophisticated means to induce people to become addicted: to feel a need and a hopeless infatuation not only for drugs and alcohol but also for chocolate, for sport — not playing it but watching it — for work, for travel, for whatever somebody else can commodify and sell. Most obedient to the system's behests is an addiction to shopping, in and of itself, no matter what is actually wanted or ends up being bought. It makes perfect sense, if one takes it as given that the only important goal is buying and selling. It has even been put to us that going shopping is, in our society, a patriotic duty; so much for permissiveness. In an addicted society, we are about as free to roam as a goat tethered to a pole: wander we may, and constantly do, but it won't get us very far. And there are consequences, always: chance is determinism, remember. The results may escape prediction, but they are ineluctable — so says the oracle of chance.

With the eclipse of Marx, among sociologists the work of Max Weber has achieved unrivalled prominence. Weber believed that in the industrialized world he was describing in the early twentieth century, the dominance of economic interests coupled with rationalism must inevitably lead to disenchantment. By "disenchantment," he meant the loss in the first place of religious belief and then of meaningful politics. People become dull — and therefore manipulable. Should any individual or group show evidence of what Weber called "charisma" and a will to raise their sights to something higher — or merely something more vivid — that new energy will inevitably become deadened by routine. Comfortlessly he pointed to the flattening effect of group understanding and the bias introduced by material interests. Even if we should struggle for salvation — as some have done — history inevitably turns our achievements into a trap. Weber, like Marx, believed in the inevitability — the fatedness — of historical processes.

Upon us has accordingly descended, Weber said, an "iron cage" — namely, rationalistic, capitalist society. He himself could not see how anybody could get out of it — not least because people learn to like their cage. For inside that cage, Freud's stern reality principle, which was supposed to impose conditions on the urge to pleasure, has actually become wedded to his pleasure principle, joining forces with it in a manner that renders us helpless. This is not a bad definition of addiction. We must be appalled, Weber wrote, but we must be resigned.[16] From chance, from sour meaninglessness, from disenchantment emerges that fatalist nightmare: a cage of iron.

Let us now take technology, fate, chance — all things mechanical and inhuman that rule us, although we ourselves both created them and gave them their power over us — let us contemplate them as one and then dream. What we behold is a new monster in the ancient tradition of gorgons, beasts, Furies, and dragons. Like a creature once known as an *egregore* (literally "out of the *grex*," or herd), this is a personification of the terrors of the group, a mythical challenge to human resourcefulness. Our modern contribution to the progeny of mythical monsters is the robot, or manmade automaton, which puts humanity on trial and even questions our definition of ourselves, as monsters always have done. An automaton, in modern English, is a creature that is similar to a living being in that it moves by itself — that is, without having to be either pushed or pulled. Human design has given birth to it (for in our generation, the consequences of resourcefulness are what demand new resourcefulness from us). But in many of our fictional narratives, the automaton now moves without any human control whatever. In ancient Greek, the word *automaton* meant not only a thing moving by itself but also causeless chance.

The horror of such a being is that it looks human, but

it isn't. It is both more invulnerable than we are (made of metal, say, and without human responses such as pity) and less complex (it moves remorselessly, because automatically, to its goal); it has no soul. Yet a robotic automaton, in many of our myths, has a pathetic side as well. The word "robot" has the same roots as the German *Arbeit*, work. The Czech and Polish word *robota* means servitude or forced labour: the creature is manufactured by human beings to do their work for them.[17]

The early robots ran amok; we feared and hated them, and our heroes had to muster all their courage to smash them before the havoc they were creating went so far that human existence was threatened by it. Nowadays, we find it more and more tempting to humanize our robots. They apologize, sometimes, for their misdemeanours; they change their minds, want to be loved, may even show more morality and sensitivity than the human characters who take part in their stories. What could this remarkable change in our dreaming mean?

Until very recently, human beings went to considerable trouble to keep it clear in their own minds that they were not animals. We learned, with not a little outrage, that we had in fact evolved gradually, from antecedents more primitive than ourselves. But still, we felt we were a higher species. A lot of emphasis, in every culture, has been laid on our notable difference from other life on earth. Today, however, we stress how similar we are — at least to animals. Science once told us that we are as near as two pins to apes. Now we have been shown that we have only twice as many genes as a fruit fly.

The truth is that we have become afraid of ourselves — afraid of our own ecological destructiveness, which has become so obvious that even the people paid to reassure us, what the French succinctly call *savants de service*, or "experts who may be called upon to say anything," can no longer conceal it from us. We therefore repeat to ourselves that we belong to the earth after all: we are not set over it or over against it. We vaguely hope that nature will turn out to be greater than we are — that although nature is nothing but a blind agglomeration of atoms, it will nevertheless impose limits upon us and prevent us from going too far. Fate and its soulmate, chance, easily come to seem kinder than is freedom. Our fictional robots, automata born of technology and inevitability, resemble animals in that they are stronger, perhaps, but otherwise only slightly, if at all, unlike us.

And where do we fit in? Here our monsters begin striking to the quick, as monsters are created and trained to do. Aren't we ourselves something like automata? There's nothing unique about us, we are constantly being told. We're also predictable, locked into our desires, governed not by our wills but by our genes, ruled by exterior forces such as society or the market. Increasingly, we talk about ourselves as "programmed" or "wired" to think and act in various ways — except that when it comes to being programmed, we are forced to admit that machines function much faster and more tirelessly than we do. They play chess better, for instance. It's easy to conclude that very often computers *know best*.

Cognitive scientists today, proponents of the so-called

second cybernetics, like using computers as analogies for human beings. The entire universe, says this theory, everything that is ordered, is on a long flight towards disintegration. One is reminded of the collapse of the vortex as imagined by the ancient Greek Atomists. Human beings occupy a surprising little pocket — short-lived and doomed — of resistance to the general entropy ("turning back" in Greek) of everything into chaos. Human beings are like machines, these scientists add, temporary ambulant systems, and what we know about how machines work can be applied to ourselves. *Artificial People and Machines with Souls* is the subtitle of a recent book on the subject.[18] Mythology, once again, is mirrored in cosmology; both express the state of human opinion about ourselves.

We spent many centuries fighting our way out of Greek and Roman beliefs that we are not free but fated. Nowadays, the official myth is still that we have never been more free. But in many ways, we are letting that freedom slip away from us; we are falling back into fate. Many, and among them the most influential of us, have ceased, apparently, to believe that "the truth shall make you free." Belief in the possibility of transcendence is dying, even though transcendent hopes and moral principles are the only sources we can draw on if we are to arrest a decline into unbridled greed, ecological devastation, and short-sighted violence. Yet neither an acceptance of iron cages and other prisons of fate nor seeking refuge in the mindless, meaningless turmoil of chance offers freedom.

In the next chapter, I shall be looking again at the linear

model of fate. What happens when that diagram provides not only a view of life as fated but also a picture of our morality?

I V

TRANSGRESSION

THE NEED OF EVERY HUMAN BEING both for free-
dom and for justice is absolute and unconditional. This is
one fact that all of us understand, even those who believe
that nature is all there is. But nature knows nothing of
freedom. It is blind and implacable; justice is nowhere to
be found in it. Yet every one of us knows what freedom
and justice are — most especially when we are deprived
of them.

I have chosen in this book to look at metaphors for fate
and their consequences. Fate is the opposite of freedom and
has nothing to do with justice. Many of its metaphors
derive from the universal propensity of human beings to
imagine time as having spatial extension: a lifetime as a
line or as a bounded area, a choice as an arrival at a crossroads, chance as the accidental intersections of lines or the
collision of dots. I've chosen to call often on Greek (and
that means also Roman) thinking about fate.

People still study the Classics in our universities

largely because of the lucidity and the vividness of Greek art and thought; the contribution of the Romans (whose intellectual mentors were the Greeks) included political lessons to be derived from imperial force, practicality, and efficiency. The Greeks and Romans are like us in that historically they are our roots and their achievements are constitutive of a great deal of our culture. They are also utterly foreign to us and therefore always thought-provoking. For we are unlike them in important respects — in some of the most important respects of all. The familiar and the strange, the brilliantly creative, the beautiful, and the utterly weird: the combination is endlessly stimulating.

What transformed the Classical world was, of course, Christianity. The new religion was born out of the profound and revolutionary insights of Judaism — its understanding that the transcendent God is one (not a company of divinities) and also good; its view of God as alive and dynamic in the world's history; its insistence on hope for the future. Christianity did not sweep the Classics away but carried them with it in its movement forward. In important respects, it turned Greek and Roman culture on its head, sometimes reversing rather than destroying its constructions.[1]

It is not my purpose in this book to explain what Christianity is. But a few examples, chosen for their relevance to my subject, may remind us of how Christianity changed our inheritance — which perdures — of the Classics. The ideals, of course, are the most important aspects of what changed. These ideals have been and still are often betrayed. But still, ideals, attitudes, and goals are as constitutive of history as are facts, misapplications, and failures. Here, then, are some examples.

Christianity, as we have already seen, substitutes guilt and forgiveness (*not* guilt alone) for honour and shame. It replaces time as cyclic and eternal recurrence (time as fate) with emergent possibility: change, discovery, hope, and liberation — the Jewish vision of Exodus. Its transcendent principles underwrite the equality of all human beings under God. They confirm universality — all nations and races, since all were created by God — and they demand respect for the uniqueness and inherent value of every single human being on earth. Christianity proclaims that liberty comes before law, and that law exists to protect liberty. It has provided a vast impetus to individualism: every one of us has a personal salvation to pursue, a personal relationship with God, a personal interiority, a responsibility for his or her own choices. It insisted from the beginning that an individual was not the occupant of a *moira* and imprisoned by fate in the shape of other people's neighbouring *moirai* but a free being of intrinsic worth and unfathomable depth, living in relationship with others while creatively engaged in the ongoing project that is his or her own life.

There was a wholly new dissociation of correct ritual from ethical offence; a rejection of the ideas of contagious pollution and ritual impurity (that is, the possibility of being contaminated merely through living close to people believed to be impure); a denial that any individual could inherit guilt from the past, or that illness could be a punishment for sin. All of these changes meant a turning away from fatalism. Christianity delegitimized sacrifice. (Powerful ancient religious ideas and social strategies such as ritual pollution, animal sacrifice, and stained purity have been so successfully superseded in Christianized cultures that most of us need to learn about them from scratch before we can perceive their logic.) Christianity put God above the emperor: only God, and never a human being or a human group, should be thought of as lord of the earth. It put love first — a shocking idea for an ancient Greek. When Nietzsche rejected Christianity, he expressed his loathing for this post-Classical religion's valorization of the weak, its insistence that the victim is right, its determination actually to champion the poor and to claim solidarity with the marginalized.

Most specifically for the subject matter of this book, Christianity proclaims that God's will is not fate but, at the deepest level, a mandate to question without restriction,[2] to revise our opinion when we find we have been misled, and then to convert and change our ways. We not only *can* change our behaviour and our political arrangements but are supposed to do so when we see we have been wrong. It is our own wrongdoing and mistakes that we should seek to change first, and not those of another person or group; Christians believe they should ask *themselves* what they have done wrong when political catastrophes occur. Conversion, or a decision to change, literally to "turn over," requires a change in the will — one's own will. Far from being fated, this can occur only in freedom: not even God can force a human being to convert. Conversion includes knowledge but goes deeper. Christians, unlike most ancient Greeks, never believe that knowledge is enough.[3] And in its rejection of honour and shame, Christianity insists that a simple person, small in the eyes of the world, might be a greater saint, a greater hero, than someone rich, famous, and brilliant.

In these and in many other ways, Christianity has, over the past two thousand years, been gradually revising its Greek and Roman heritage. The Greeks believed in fate and thought about it deeply. The metaphors they used are worth considering carefully, because they are powerful, still operative, and can be dangerous unless they are used with conscious vigilance. It is my belief that, in the West at any rate, to the precise degree that we fall away from Christianity (from Christian ideals, I mean, not from betrayals of those ideals), we fall back into fatalist thinking. We give up our important and hard-won freedom and responsibility for our own actions, although an inborn yearning for freedom sometimes leads us to tell ourselves that what we are doing is achieving an escape. We don't call our loss of freedom fate, necessarily — we give it other names, such as inevitability, or predisposition, or helplessness, or even obligation.

I said earlier that fate has nothing to do with justice. Yet the diagram of fate as portion was and is commonly used to express morality. When this happens, justice can become, almost self-evidently, a matter of revenge for wrongs done. When used for ethical purposes, the diagram most obviously expresses honour and shame, which are always either infected or actually inspired by a belief in fate. The point is that we find it easy and natural to think about concepts such as time, or to imagine social arrangements, while referring to the spatial picture that I call the fatal diagram — but we had better be careful when we do so, because mistakes can arise almost unconsciously from its use. The diagram can cause slippage both into honour and shame and into fatalist thinking. Leaving the diagram, on the other hand, and replacing it with nothing leads to meaninglessness. Fate and meaninglessness are equal though opposite temptations, to be understood as two sides of the same coin. Leave out transcendence, leave out forgiveness, and you get one or the other, or both.

I shall illustrate what I mean by looking again at ancient Greek attitudes, this time towards morality as well as fate. *Hamartia* and *hybris* were how the Greeks conceived of sin. *Hamartia* was a scarcely moral concept; it was not a question of guilt. What it meant most essentially was making a mistake, aiming at something and missing the target, falling into error. (*Error*, a Latin word, means wandering, leaving the beaten path — beaten because correct — and getting lost.) *Hybris* was transgression — deliberate or not, it hardly mattered. It involved crossing a boundary ("transgression," in Latin, means stepping over).

The Furies, handmaids of fate, responded to such an action, whether it had been intentional or not, with one — or both — of two punishments: either they tied the transgressor up or they pursued him, forcing him to flee from them in terror. The hybristic sinner, as spoiler of the pattern of bounded areas that was fate, was made to pay by being tied up in ropes — lines that confined his body, rendering him incapable of movement. The Furies might, on the other hand, drive the transgressor mad, chasing him away from the sheltering city walls, away from the map of streets and all the city's other structures, and out across a featureless plain. Madness was confusion, a loss of points of reference. The punishments of the Furies were claustrophobia and agoraphobia: either the diagram, its boundaries enforced, or an exhausting pursuit across flat and meaningless space.

The ancient Greek diagram of fate saw human lives as portions of a society conceived as a limited whole. Shame kept people within bounds. The god Apollo had ten commandments, the first two of which were "Know thyself" and "Nothing too much." These were two aspects of one wisdom: know your limits, but know also your extent (that is, how far you can possibly go). The other Delphic commandments were: Curb thy spirit; Go as far as the limit; Hate hybris; Keep a reverent tongue; Fear authority; Bow before the divine; Boast not of strength; Keep woman under rule.[4] Honour demanded that each person, each *moira* or portion, should fight always to be as large or as considerable as possible in the view of others. Shame, meanwhile, insisted on limits. Areas fought the lines that enclosed them; each *moira*, each amount of honour, was in competition against every other, and especially against those close to or contingent with it. "Rivalry" is a word that derives from the idea of a boundary, here a *rivus*, Latin for a riverbank: rivals are people with a common boundary. Wisdom was knowing precisely how much power one could exert.

The boundaries, as rules will, broke often — under stress, under a want of wisdom. Somebody would invade his neighbour's portion of honour — he would move his own limiting line, as it were, outwards, to his own advantage. Because of the notion of limited goods, such an incursion represented a takeover.[5] The reduction of a contingent *moira* meant the addition of that amount of honour to one's own portion. Instantly, the reduced one fought back: he had to. Revenge was the appropriate response where honour had been lost; the reaction was as inevitable as fate. The model was that of invasion, despoiling by an enemy, occupation — and its result, its ineluctable result, was warfare.

Ancient Greeks had no conundrum corresponding to the Christian and Jewish problem of evil. To begin with, their gods were not good — they were merely magnificent and powerful. Greeks knew that the result of *hybris* — stepping over — was, necessarily, disorder. If somebody jostled the pattern, everyone was forced to move, and probably to suffer. Voids were created, and they cried out to be filled: a struggle had to take place, with each one looking out for his own interests. Belief in fate meant that it was not only the result of *hybris* that had to ensue, but that the first overweening or presumptuous act was itself fated. The universe itself, Greek thinkers surmised, came to be out of boundlessness; but thenceforward it is by necessity a battleground, where life is movement but movement is *hybris*, and *hybris* always demands revenge.

Hybris for them was there at, and in fact a root cause of, the coming-to-be of the world.[6] Human beings, as we have noted before, frequently project their own social attitudes and arrangements into their visions of how the universe operates.

An invaded neighbour, then, fought back to restore order, in the shape of his own honour, with all the power at his command. This neighbour was almost invariably a man, for women seldom fight over honour in such a system. Women are honour personified, whereas it is the duty of men to guard honour, which in important respects is represented by the purity and irreproachability of their women. Women were often metaphorically described as "land" to be "ploughed" by men. Adultery, rape, and abduction were seen in ancient Greece less as sexual crimes than as the removal of a woman from a man, taking with her his honour. The Trojan War began when Helen was abducted from her husband and taken off to Troy.

If a man, then, whose honour had been reduced could not take it back from his attacker, he looked elsewhere for a replacement. He invaded — shamed, reduced — some other man's honour instead, adding that, of course, to his own. And so the trouble spread, like a raging fire or boat crashing against boat in a tempest at sea: both images were used to describe this horrifying spread of disorder and destruction. Pretty soon, people were suffering — many of them innocent, many of them having no idea what started the upheaval in the first place. Meanwhile, the gods looked on, loving the drama of it all, discussing the events with interest, watching fate unfold. They were chiefly concerned for their own honour, which was represented by the heroes they favoured.

The Greeks had a word for the results of *hybris*. It was *até*. *Até* was disorder — not only disorder after and as a result of *hybris*, but also disorder beforehand, causing *hybris*. (*Hybris*, of course, was itself fated: fate turns effects into causes, as well as causes into inevitable effects.) For a person to commit *hybris*, to decide to enlarge himself at the expense of his neighbour, he must first be crazy — fail to know himself, be prepared to go too far. He breaks the first two commandments of Apollo, not thinking of the gravity of what he is doing or being too far gone to care. We ourselves still have expressions describing a person in a state of incipient *hybris* — or in the process of committing it. He is "too big for his boots," we say. He is puffed up with pride and certainty of success, outrageous, or overweening; he "plumes himself" — meaning he adds a feather to his height. He is "cocky" (we used to call such a person a coxcomb), meaning that he has raised his crest as a cock does when he is aggressive, making himself bigger, intending to frighten his enemy with his erect red comb. Someone who has been put down, on the other hand, we describe as "crestfallen."

It is typical, in an arena defined by honour and shame, to wish to make oneself *physically* bigger, symbolically to signify one's newly claimed extra honour. One hybristic gesture is that of sticking out one's tongue at somebody: piercing his or her area, as it were (and, in order to do it, rudely displaying something that we are taught to wish other people would keep private: a sudden, slimy tongue). An insolent or outrageous act is classed as hybristic, and it prompts others to cut the offender "down to size." In order to punish a criminal, you might kill him and reduce him in one movement: you cut off his head. Livy[7] tells how a certain king gave a sign that the time had come for his enemies to be destroyed: he said not a word but went out into his garden and slashed with his cane at the tallest poppies, decapitating them, spoiling their pride. Enemies can be reduced and shamed by cutting off their hair, as is still commonly done to collaborators after a war. Women especially have been shamed in this manner. In beard-wearing honour cultures, cutting off a man's beard, or cutting off part of it, can impose a shame past bearing. Naturally, the honour-and-shame response is to take back your honour, go after the invader, the one who has despised and derided you, and make him pay — simultaneously, no doubt, spreading *até* far and wide, causing suffering to people who are in no way to blame.

A favourite Greek metaphor for *hybris* and *até* is eating too much. A person feels hungry and eats. So far, so good. He stretches out his hand for more. Our hybristic man has already achieved what was called *koros*, one meaning for which was "satiety," enough. But having enough is not the end of his self-extension: *koros* can also mean "too much." The man is greedy — a form of "*até* before the event." He eats more — and more. Finally, he throws up. A foul mess, disgust, revulsion: *até*. Rather as in a war, *hybris* exacts revenge — and then all hell breaks loose.

Rape was *hybris* — invading the boundary of another's

body, violating his or her purity, causing (in a culture dedicated to honour) not only shame to the entire family, but in a woman permanent diminishment. A raped woman — innocent though she may be — might never be thought worthy of marriage again; a married woman was, after all, her husband's honour personified, and no man wanted "spoiled goods" embodying his honour. Shame is not guilt; it cannot be forgiven. Shame is reduction: no more — but also no less. Murder was *hybris*, of course — stabbing, dismembering. In ancient Greece, stabbing was an acceptable method of both killing and suicide for men, a dagger being appropriately phallic and hybristic. Women often chose poison, partly because women were the preparers and servers of food. And besides, murdering someone by poisoning his or her food was sneaky, deceptive behaviour, and so typical of women, unlike the straightforward, declarative, courageous male action of drawing one's sword. Women committing suicide often chose hanging. Here the symbolism was that of the outline of fate, *anangké*: the line around the universe, the walls around the city, the boundary of the house, the body's outline, the noose around the neck.

The Furies, as servants of fate, saw to it that *hybris* never went unpunished. Their responses were inevitable, as automatic as fate. They inhabited the lines of the system, much as an electric current lives in a wire fence, delivering shocks to any person or animal that attempts to cross it. Christopher Robin, the hero of *When We Were Very Young*, knew all about guardian monsters, in his case

> the masses of Bears
> Who wait at the corners all ready to eat
> The sillies who tread on the lines of the street ... [8]

Zeus, king of the gods, also protected boundaries with his thunderbolt. He blasted hybristic warriors as they climbed the walls of cities they were invading and people blasphemously leaping over the walls of sanctuaries, areas they had no business entering. Such walls were built to keep other people *out*. They were for protection, and protection, like the law, needs "teeth" to keep it operating. The Furies, therefore, were useful fiends. Aeschylus shows us in his trilogy, *The Oresteia*, that the ancient black and bloody Furies were in fact needed by the city. When nobody was troubling the boundaries, the Furies were quiet. Then people called them Eumenides, the Kindly Ones. They were aroused to anger, changed colour, and issued forth from their holes in the ground only when somebody was interfering with the most essential of the culture's categories. These included the stable structure of taboos against incest and kin murder, the inviolable protection provided by a sanctuary, the mighty obligations — "obligation" means binding — entered into when taking an oath. (Oaths, too, were encircling lines; we still say we can "break" an oath, just as we may "release" someone from a promise.) The Furies were kindly; the Furies were merciless. There are two sides to every fence.

In the diagram of contingent *moirai*, each one pressing against those surrounding it, every boundary both allows and limits the area within it. Next, it protects that space from intrusion from without. We have noted before that such a system relies not only on power but also on already existing categories. Truth, for the ancient Greeks, tended to be synonymous with What Is and the beauty of What Is, and What Is was fated. The areas were each man's portion of the honour that was bestowed upon him by others, and it was his responsibility to maintain the amount of it — indeed, to increase it if at all possible. It was to be fought for and protected from reduction or defilement, as was the honour of women, of family, and of country.

The ancient Greeks themselves did seek ways out of the trap set by the diagram of honour and shame and of fate. It was they, after all, who began to imagine the transcendent ideal of democracy. They invented trial by jury. And in their drama and poetry they created heroes, part of whose mission was always to introduce new life and possibility into the fatal grid: even though the grid always won, the hero remained heroic as he embraced his fate. But the spatial picture continued to be basic. It is so powerful and primordial a metaphor that it still survives at the backs of our own minds; the same meanings adhere to it whenever we fall back into believing that force is all and transcendence impossible. We also continue to press the diagram into service as a theorem demonstrating morality. For example, we use it as a picture of aspects of what we mean by human rights. Here the lines of something resembling a grid represent protection for each person from every other by means of the law.

"And now I will tell a fable for princes who themselves understand," wrote the poet Hesiod in about 700 B.C.:

> Thus said the hawk to the nightingale with speckled neck, while he carried her high up among the clouds, gripped fast in his talons, and she, pierced by his crooked claws, cried pitifully. To her he spoke disdainfully: "Miserable thing, why do you cry out? One far stronger than you now holds you fast, and you must go wherever I take you, no matter how well you can sing. I will either make my meal of you — or let you go: it depends on how I feel. He is a fool who tries to withstand the stronger, for he does not get the mastery, and suffers pain besides his shame." So said the swiftly flying hawk, the long-winged bird.[9]

In nature, Hesiod's fable tells us, might is right. And so it is in human society, unless something utterly different from force is allowed to rule. The abbé Guyot Desfontaines was once questioned by the powerful comte d'Argenson about a dangerously satirical essay he had written. "But I write for a living," protested the abbé. "I have to live!" "I don't see why," replied the count, with implacable *froideur*.[10] Let us say it was a clash of opinions; the count, naturally, thought that his counted for more. Nothing on earth, nothing in nature, could protect the little writer from the wrath of the great man if it were not for something utterly *un*natural — a realization that an admiration for justice and fairness, rather than power, is what makes us truly human.

No one of us is a match for a crowd of others — not in

nature, at any rate. The notion of human rights contra-
dicts the axioms that big exceeds small, that many are
more than one. Instead, we dare to proclaim the ideal that
One is as important as Many, and for that reason many
should not prevail over the rights of one. Each one is a
bearer of rights and is permitted by law to claim his or her
rights, just as democracy gives each member of society a
vote. Rights help people to help themselves. They also
lead rights-bearers to see others as having rights as well.[11]
For human rights, like the notion of equality, like democracy itself, are based upon transcendence, upon an
aspiration to rise above the dominions both of power and
of fate. We have to admit that no effective means of
enforcing rights has yet been found — especially when
they are most under threat, where there is no respect for
law. But that fact in no way diminishes the aspiration.
And we are not afraid of going against nature in all of
this. We know perfectly well that it is the nature of
human beings to oppose nature when something higher
is at stake. However, neither democracy nor human
rights are natural, and therefore the struggle for them is
never-ending: both of them are projects, ongoing.

In some respects, modern demands for human rights
are unswerving. The first two inalienable rights, for
instance — that to life and that to freedom — permit no
degrees of fault: we demand that they be upheld, right
now and without prevarication. People are absolutely
not to be tortured, arbitrarily imprisoned, executed.
There are to be no condemnations in secret, no kangaroo
courts, no blackmail. Human rights most readily formu-

late themselves as prohibitions: fences keep intruders out. There are supposed to be no gradations with rights — no picking and choosing who is to qualify. A violation is a violation, even if it happens only once. And feelings or tastes in these matters make no difference whatever. The Furies themselves could not be more implacable.

But because of our aspiration to rise above honour and shame and fate, and in a spirit utterly unlike that of the Furies of ancient Greece, we are prepared to qualify the very rules we have made. We do not, for example, punish people who did not intend to break the rules, or those who did so accidentally. As long as the ideals upon which our culture was founded are allowed to survive, we shall find it possible to pardon people who are sorry and make reparations. And we shall insist that punishment ought never to be meted out in revenge. The metaphorical diagram is still used to depict human rights as outlines demanding inviolability, however, and we have to remember that fate haunts it. A continued preference for merciful and just interpretations of the diagram can never be taken for granted. Such a preference is transcendent, not natural, and it's certainly not part of the diagram. It is therefore to be fought for with all the energy at our command, or else we shall fall back into fate.

I have been speaking mainly of the *lines* in the picture of rights. What about the areas they enclose? For the ancient Greeks, what filled those spaces was an immensely lively and noble desire to be honourable, to live to the full one's portion in life, to be seen by others to be what one was: magnificent. The honour system made the presence of other people in one's life a *sine qua non*; they had to be satisfied, and if possible impressed, by one's virtue, and honour provided a powerful drive to give them reasons to be admiring. What fills the areas in the diagram as a metaphor for human rights? All lines and nothing meaningful to live up to or to protect is a recipe for emptiness and futility — which themselves are a version of fate.

One mistake we often make, in our pride in human rights as an ideal, is to behave as though they were all we need — as though they could be extended to cover everything. We demand of them that they should go beyond rules and immunities. It has been suggested, for example, that charters of obligations should supplement charters of rights[12]; indeed, obligations can truthfully be called primary.[13] It is also sometimes said that a language of needs should replace talk of rights, and certainly needs are represented by some of the space in the diagram. People cannot be free — and will not survive — if they have no food, no housing, no jobs, no adequate education.

Human rights, however, merely create conditions under which free choices can be made without fear of unwarranted pressures or limitations from other people, provided that those choices do not subtract from the rights of others. Human rights are not deciders of what should be done or directors of what choices shall be made. Rights in some ways resemble polite manners, which is why they commonly give rise to political correctness: they can demand, provided we are law-abiding, that we should behave as though we recognize the worth of others; they cannot instil in us genuine regard for anyone. Conditions for action are negative in character; they are not themselves actions. Diagrammatically speaking, lines regulate, protect, and delimit; areas are something else entirely.

The idea of rights, partly because our fatal diagram consists of fences as in a map of farmers' fields, is modelled on the idea of property: "my" rights. Careless use of the diagram further encourages this metaphor of property: each segment enclosed by a line, which is supposed to represent a human person in all of his or her depth, complexity, and freedom, deteriorates into something resembling a flat and passive piece of land, an area with a certain size. Violation of rights therefore turns easily into a form of *hybris*, the prime metaphor for which is the invasion of a country's borders, or efforts to move or to ignore the fences around a neighbour's land. People then make human rights claims as though somebody else were treading on "my space." Litigation becomes a warlike retaliation for an invasion.

And the habit of litigation should remind us that human rights can become what they are ideally meant to oppose: expressions of power and force. Rights provide individual persons, and sometimes groups, with support in the face of injustice — originally, and still in many cases, the injustice of the state. But to treat rights as a battleground among rival claimants to a limited good, especially when what is sought is one's own increase at the expense of the rights of others, is eventually to regress into containment by that flat and purely horizontal diagram, with no vertical dimension, nothing that goes beyond struggles for power. Rival claims to rights require an overview, which implies — in an admittedly spatial metaphor — "going up higher"; they need wisdom in a search for overall balance and fairness. Deny the transcendent overview, and you fall back first into force and then into fate. Human rights are essential to any possibility of justice in the modern world. But they can't be all there is. They are not enough.

The problem with the image of a grid that we have been looking at is that movement within it must of necessity involve transgression. No movement, even where the grid has achieved consent and a degree of fairness, is, for human beings, a form of death. There are always factors that have not been taken into account — new dangers, new ideas, new insights. It is often entirely necessary that transgression should take place.

This benign transgression occurs when a person or a group rises up and changes the way we see things: a new story begins to be told. Mythically speaking, such a clarification of issues, and the introduction of new life to the dull grid, is performed by what is called a hero. All stories revolve around heroes — they always have done, and they still do: each one of us, after all, is the hero of a life lived, of dreams dreamed. But heroism, understood from without, is always partly mythical. For the facts, even about real heroes, are often bent in the service of the story being told: insofar as a person is a hero, the story is more important than the facts.

Heroes are created to represent us, as human beings

who have to contend with the fatal diagram, to live with it but also to transcend it. Heroes are transgressive figures by nature.[14] Their purpose is to shake us up. They are, to begin with, larger than the rest of us; a hero must tread on other people's toes just to be what he is. His new wisdom he has to find from "beyond" us — and typically the story presents the hero as undertaking a quest, a wandering, outside the grid entirely. A hero may leave behind the whole tight diagram, transgress even the outline that holds it all together: *anangké*, the "fetter" called necessity. Having found out there what was missing and necessary, or having killed the monster crouching in the outer darkness and threatening us all, he comes back home. He *must* come home, cross back over that outer wall, and return to us bearing his gifts.

Because the hero is a boundary-crosser, he is also hybristic: he has to be, or he could not carry out his function. The logic of the diagram then insists that he must pay. Heroes suffer; they frequently die, often put to death by us. But even in such a case, to be a hero is to have done what we needed done: he has clarified something for us, found an answer, discovered a new and fruitful direction that we desperately needed. Heroic transgression is never just mindless disobedience. If a hero transgresses, it is in order to deepen and broaden the best in us, not to spoil or obliterate it. His actions are principled and clear enough for us to understand them, even if we never entirely get our minds around him. A hero is energy personified, since it is his duty to reinvigorate his society. He is extraordinary, a man of honour rather than of common sense. For common sense is cautious and limiting; it is also merely common.

Heroes are always, in a sense, born out of honour and shame. The reason is that we — the many — are essential to the hero's story. We make room for him, allow him to take up more "space" than other people. And it is we who crown him with hero status; that is why he has got to care enough about us to come home to us. A hero who goes "out there" and never comes back tends simply to be forgotten by us, the hero-makers. Heroes need to be *remembered*: the survival of the benefits they brought us depends on our remembering. And we have, at the very least, to know what it is the hero has done — otherwise how can we decide, amazed, that he is a hero? (I keep speaking of heroes as males. As we saw earlier, the honour-and-shame system is mainly about the actions of men; but women make especially powerful heroes. We'll look at the example of Antigone a little later.)

I have said that it is the project of our culture to transcend honour and shame, to correct that system and rise above it if we can. But honour and shame are not always bad; they will certainly always exert themselves among us. The modern phenomenon of spectator sport is one obvious space we have created to enjoy honour and shame as spectacle. Huge numbers of people — we, the many — gather to watch the heroic few battle it out so that we can sift out the truly great from the merely excellent. The drama is played out before our eyes so that we can judge, take sides, see *hybris* performed as it must be by heroes.

Many games are about lines and the crossing of lines and barriers; if there is an object fought over, it is often a ball, round as the universe, round as Truth in the vision of Parmenides. Competitive sports often take place in an arena, bounded with an outline like fate and so suggestive of combat that the word "arena" is used figuratively for any sphere of public action. There are goals, heights and lengths to be surpassed, clear winners, fatal rules, implacable timing devices and their guardians, the umpires and judges. The winners get the treasure: the medals in their hierarchy of honour (good, better, best), the huge golden cup. (A cup or a dish, as a measure, is an ancient metaphor for fate as portion.) The spectators who have backed the winners hoist their heroes high on their shoulders, and the city as a whole goes wild — or at least is made as aware as possible of the triumph; there is plenty of spurting, phallic, transgressive champagne.

It is important, however, to understand that our culture has relegated all this honour and shame to a clearing especially prepared for it. The point about sport performed before a watching crowd is truly its unimportance, its character as something ephemeral, as a safety valve. The pleasure is very real, the achievements amazing, but in the end, this is honour and shame, and as such cannot take over our lives — not, at least, the lives of the spectators. These are merely games, and they cannot — or shouldn't — really matter.

Because all of us — the people who are not heroic — are spectators who contemplate our heroes and their narratives, watch their actions, and gauge their prowess, these great beings must be easy to recognize; the hero has a simple and unmistakable image. This does not mean that the hero's message is simple; in stories that last in our minds, it almost never is. But there must be a clarity about this person, who has both to be known to the many and to clarify problems for them. The figure has to be different from other people, too, and he often expresses this singularity by means of some physical oddity. A hero will have holes in his ankles like Oedipus, be unbelievably strong, rowdy, and sexy like Hercules or tiny and smart like Tom Thumb. A scar by which he may be recognized is always useful.

In the modern world, well-known figures — "celebrities," from the Latin word *celeber*, meaning much frequented — often have talismanic characteristics: Marilyn Monroe's smile and beauty spot and blonde bob; Glenn Gould's greatcoat and mittens; Beethoven's thunderous face and his deafness; Hitler's lick of hair and his moustache. (Oh yes, villains usually grope for heroic status; a whole department of hero studies could be devoted to them. They want followers, after all — in other words, us. And heroes in the first instance, in the original honour-and-shame pattern, are about size and power, not goodness.)

A troubling aspect of today's celebrities is the extent to which they are *given* to us; we rarely have the opportunity to create them or to find them for ourselves. Sports figures at least have to prove themselves; for that reason alone, sport can seem, on some TV nights, almost the only reality available. Celebrities, on the other hand, can be famous merely for being famous. Modern celebrities are frequently all image and often intended merely to distract us, to fill the air with noise — and to prevent us from having our own ideas about whom to admire. Of course, in a sense we always have the last word because not even a publicity campaign can ensure that we shall accept someone as heroic, at least not for any length of time. And it is only we, the many, who are able to grant someone hero status. Still, it is disturbing and finally degrading, an aspect of the meaninglessness I described in my last chapter, that we should be bombarded with ready-made images of false heroes — who are useful, often, merely for making us buy things — to the point where we have no energy left to think for ourselves about who we really admire, or, indeed, who we are or aspire to be.

Fate plays a role in many heroic legends. Oedipus *must* kill the Sphinx because the prize is the queen, his mother, whom he is fated to marry. The word "sphinx" in Greek, cognate with "sphincter," is from *sphingo*, meaning "I clutch" or "I strangle." She is herself a version of necessity, the tight outline that is the periphery of the universe. Like the Furies and other monsters embodying fate, the Sphinx is a mixed creature, in her case part woman, part lion. When Oedipus answers the riddle and destroys the monster, he thinks that he is liberating a foreign city called Thebes; but in fact, killing the fatal Sphinx allows him to go home, as heroes must — home to complete his fate. He had murdered his father "at the place where the three roads meet" — the crossroads, the junction of choice. Having killed the obstructive stranger, his father, he had felt "free" — to take the fatal road home, to encounter the Sphinx, and so to win his mother for his bride, as the Oracle of Apollo had foretold.

The heroic pattern is known to us through our experience of the stories and legends of our culture. It is we, after all, who tell these stories and listen to them. But the most important point about the pattern is that it is known *in order that it might be altered*. Similarly, we may keep and use the diagram — provided that we can transcend it. Every story, every fiction, is a meditation on what it is to be heroic; it offers its insights through *differences* from the pattern. Often the premise is this: Here is a person who looks unheroic, someone so innocent as to appear either stupid or far too clever (to be "smart" has something unheroic about it: intelligence is acceptable, but ingenuity or even complexity problematic); someone with inadequate or missing parents, with a terrible deed in his past, or who is confined to his apartment with a broken leg but nevertheless contrives to save the day. Women have traditionally tended to be disqualified from famous exploits and fitted into the honour-and-shame pattern mainly in passive roles. Yet a woman could be a hero, for one of the aims of a story has always been to force readers and listeners to admit that an unlikely candidate for heroism *is* in fact a hero. The story takes place in the gap between this figure and the pattern.

Odysseus, "the man of many wiles," who lacks that archetypal heroic attribute, simplicity, nevertheless makes his long journey home with single-hearted desire, kills the greedy and hybristic men who are after his wife, and sets his house to rights. Antigone, a young girl, a weak female, defies the king in the name of transcendent justice, as many a Christian martyr was later to do. She has insisted on carrying out the forbidden burial of the corpse of the traitor, who happened to be her dead brother. Burial for the dead is care for those who can no longer fight on their own behalf: Antigone's action is utterly without self-interest. Knowing the consequences of defying the king's decree, she makes a journey out to achieve this deed (although women were supposed to stay in the house) and insists on publicity for her action (although women were expected to shun publicity). Otherwise how will people know what she has done and see that she, and not the king, is the hero? She dies, put to death by Kreon, and so reveals the importance to Thebes of laws that lie outside the jurisdiction of the state.[15]

Transgression is the stuff of stories and characteristic of their heroes. But transgression in itself is either simply destructive or constitutes a merely horizontal movement across boundaries. Even the heroic quest out into "what lies beyond" and then the return home might serve only to feed the system of contingent *moirai* lying snugly within its fatal outline. The story's author has to add a whole new dimension to the hero's journey, aspects altogether deeper and higher, in order to communicate something of importance, and so respond to the demands of the audience that they be "shaken up."

Stories about heroes take up the pattern, the grid of *moirai*, and not only people it, and so bring it to life, but also transcend it, or use it for transcendent purposes.

They may show, for example, that "little" people can in fact be understood to be great. (This is the message of thousands of stories about saints in many religions; it is also the theme of countless novels.) Courage is found to exist where people tend not to look for it; love is greater than death, poor people nobler than rich ones, beauty discovered in something very simple or ordinary.

The creativity expended in telling stories is immensely rich; stories are the treasure hoards of the human race. Usually they depend on the juxtaposition of the original model — the heroic pattern — with a new version of it, in which twists or variations from the original reveal something surprising, something new, something moving. This is how stories win our approval: they satisfy our longing for meaning, for hope, and for transcendence. The metaphor for fate and force that we have been discussing does not disappear with this satisfaction. It stays — but we have moved beyond it. Fate has become only part of the story.

V

BEYOND FATE

IN A MOMENT OF DESPAIR, Tennyson in his poem *In Memoriam* not only characterizes nature as "red in tooth and claw" but dismisses life itself as futile. Nature delivers a "hideous 'No'" to all human aspiration towards something higher than itself, to human trust that "God was love indeed, and love Creation's final law." And this "hideous 'No'" is immediately, and typically, linked in the poem to the metaphors for fate that I have been considering: remorseless imprisonment within the lines of the pattern on the one hand, and the meaningless futility of flying particles on the other. For the human being, sundered at this point in the poem from love, hope, and faith, Tennyson's "Nature" offers two choices, and only two:

> Be blown about the desert dust
> Or seal'd within the iron hills.[1]

In the twenty-first century, "Nature red in tooth and

claw" has become more than ever a fatal monster. It offers "at bottom no design, no purpose, no evil, and no good, nothing but blind, pitiless indifference." We ourselves are merely DNA (that is, strings of sugar and phosphate molecules in double-helix shape), and "DNA neither cares nor knows," insists the zoologist Richard Dawkins. "DNA just is."[2] By putting it this way, Dawkins is giving us a picture of fate for our times. *Moira*, the pattern of doom for the ancient Greeks, also exhibited no purpose and no transcendence; it just was. Chance offered an escape from the prison of *moira* because at least it allowed movement — until it was found to be but an aspect of fate.[3] Chance, to use the words of Dawkins, was blind, pitiless, indifferent; convention spoke then, and still speaks, of chance as blind. A gene is a linear sequence of DNA, and modern knowledge of this implies, or so we are told, that we are genetically determined: a simplistic interpretation has turned biology into a version of fate.

Genes, despite scientific protests to the contrary, are persistently pictured in the media and in the minds of many people as *things*, on an analogy with atoms. Genes are even thought of as though they were agents: individual, distinct, and causal. A gene is in fact a sequence rather than a physical object.[4] It forms a tiny part of the dynamics of a complex, self-correcting living system that, in the case of a human self, has a will of its own. A gene is the encoding of a polypeptide, no more. There is no reason whatever to suppose that the most meticulous inspection of our chromosomes will either explain or absolve any one of our decisions — let alone that genes choose for themselves as if they were little persons, blind, pitiless, and "selfish."[5] Yet imagining them as though they were has become common, in part because of the ancient pictures that underlie fatalism.

Fate metaphors are constantly used for thinking about genes. Human beings are said to be "programmed," with patterns — will-governing patterns — inscribed or pre-scribed by heredity in their DNA. People are spoken of as "wired" to think in certain ways. We hear of switches and tracks, underlying networks and blueprints — fate metaphors all. James Watson, the co-discoverer of DNA, recently said that "it's a language written in four letters — [A, C, G, T] — and we have the book."[6] What we do with this four-letter "book," however, is an entirely different matter, which it is not the province of scientists to decide. (Meanwhile, there are far more interesting mysteries emerging. One is the recent realization that genes appar-ently evolved redundancy as insurance against the loss of genetic information. Evolution, we used to think, *loses* redundancy. And chance has apparently evolved, in us, a brilliantly efficient means of defeating chance.) Genes, as concepts, are in fact deeply paradoxical: they both change and conserve; they show direction as well as redundancy. The organisms they constitute are both stable and muta-ble, passive and motors of change.

But for many people, genes have mostly turned out to be a giant put-down; human beings once thought they were remarkable among nature's progeny. Genetics having recently shown us that we have more of the ani-mal in us than we were previously able to quantify, the conclusion is drawn that we must be mastered — that is, fatally driven — by instincts to the same extent that animals are. Yet we are well aware that whereas we cannot hold animals to account for their behaviour, we certainly can demand responsibility from human beings. In light of the discovery that, genetically speaking, human races are alike, we might have resolved to set aside our racist prejudices. Instead, there are terrifying spectres of new (or not so new) kinds of racism, as proposals are made for the modification of fetuses to their parents' specifications or suggestions put forward that people should provide gene profiles of themselves before being hired to do a job.[7]

Some people conclude that all social behaviour depends on our genes; genetically based neurophysical operators within the brain are supposed to compel human beings to think in certain ways. As a result, delinquency can be believed to derive from biological predestination, and parents blamed for handing on "a bad gene."[8] There are assumed to be genes for this and genes for that: for egotism, for altruism, for sexism, even a gene for monogamy, the so-called perfect husband gene.[9] Religious faith, because it is a natural human response to experience and has further been diagnosed as on the whole useful for societal well-being, must therefore depend on genes; we are told that the hunt is on for "a gene for religion." We are promised that one day we shall be able to pull a CD out of a pocket and say, "Here is a human being. It's me."[10]

A Greek myth about fate has a hero whose *moira* resided in a log of wood. His mother kept the log safe in a chest — until the day her son infuriated her by murdering his uncles, her brothers. She threw the log of wood onto a fire, and her absent son died immediately.[11] Other Greek myths portray fate as a thread spun by the Moirai; a necklace that forces its owners to bring down upon themselves an inherited doom; a wall that must inevitably be crossed, but that arouses Zeus to blast with his thunderbolt the man committing *hybris* by climbing it.[12] At least the Greeks gave us more thrilling and amusing myths about fate than that of a man embodied by a compact disc that he carries in his pocket.

The pity is that an enormous leap forward in scientific knowledge should be turned into yet another primitive version of the age-old temptation to believe in fate. It should be admitted, moreover, that scientists themselves — disgusted as they say they are by popular misconceptions — must accept a large measure of the blame. Scientists have been guilty of falling for the triumph of their success, and for the money to be made from genetic research and its promise of practical applications. But even more important, they have — or so it seems from the outside — been guilty of contempt for religion and for culture, a matter I shall discuss shortly. There are, meanwhile, really profound questions to be probed. For example, why should scientists assume that occurrences on higher ontological levels — the human moral conscience, for example — depend entirely on laws governing our underlying physical structure? Why is life on earth complex, given that biological complexity is unnecessary, hard for nature to achieve, and by no means inevitable? What, in particular, gave rise to the fact that human beings are in so many respects unique?[13]

The laws of nature and the predictability of their results, however, are what science investigates, and all that science investigates. Because science easily seems to be the only trustworthy endeavour left after the brutalities and the disappointments inflicted by ideologies and politics during the twentieth century, people often feel that we should never permit ourselves to enquire beyond the specificities of scientific experimentation. That leaves out morality, purpose, direction, even hope. Indeed, part of the attraction of asking for no more than scientific explanations is the fact that science cannot speak about moral principles. Freedom boils down, in many modern minds, to not being told what to do, so that anything resembling a principled commitment seems to be nothing but an infringement of liberty.

As far as fatalist prediction goes, we are far closer to predicting somebody's fate if we know her postal code than if we map her genes[14]: what neighbourhood you live in and what your country and social class is — that is, how much opportunity the ambient culture offers you to better your lot — are massively important factors in anybody's life. And even these cannot account in detail for any human being's actual behaviour.

Genetics, in other words, is first isolated and given overriding importance. Next, it is used irresponsibly, to reinforce existing prejudices and to invite people to think they cannot alter their behaviour, their choices, their moral directions, or their social arrangements. What we have learned about genes is made to erode our belief in freedom and to encourage fatalism.

I propose again to have recourse to ancient Greek habits of thinking in order to describe some of what I believe is happening. Early Greek philosophers, as I have mentioned before, often said that the world is made up of opposites. What we see around us are the opposites in tension: up and down, hot and cold, wet and dry, and so on. You cannot have up, they said, if you have no down. Light is meaningless without dark, and heaviness nothing unless there is lightness. In nature, the opposites were at war with one another: in a human body, for example, hot may encroach upon cold, committing *hybris* against its opposite in order to express itself — for example, as a fever. Bodily health, then, involved balance, keeping the opposites in pure and equal tension.

The great opposites were collected, discussed, listed. There were ten essential ones, for example, in the system of the Pythagoreans: limit and no limit, odd and even, one and many, right and left, male and female, motion and rest, straight and curved, light and dark, good and bad, and — last but not least — square and oblong.[15] Being simply manifestations of nature, the opposites were supposed to be value-free. In some respects, seeing things in terms of opposites was the Greeks' way of discussing the manner in which "everything is relative."

Mystics arose, as mystics tend to do, and they denied that the opposites were different. "The way up and the way down are the same," proclaimed Heraclitus[16] (and they are, if you picture a slanting line or a road in space and imagine people walking both up and down upon it). "Sea water is very pure and very impure"[17] (depending, of course, on whether you are a man or a fish, swimming in the water or drinking it). And further, "Changing, it rests"[18]: the world, as we would put it, is static and dynamic at one and the same time. Parmenides, meanwhile, denied the evidence of our senses: many and movement do not exist, he said. Being, of necessity, is one and still. Change cannot happen, for there is no coming into being or passing away, no more and no less.[19]

Apart from the difficult affirmations of mystics, discussion of "the way things are" in terms of opposites frequently meant that lists of them would be set out in columns. In this manner, the opposites constituted another fatal diagram, this time a dualist system with an imaginary vertical line dividing one column from its counterpart. Where a linear diagram put things together and provided a picture of the way things are, the opposites, disposed in columns, divided reality out or analysed it. When this happened, however, everything in one column became linked, implicitly, to everything else in that column. And it becomes clear to us — it was not always so clear to the ancient Greeks — that the opposites were not equal at all.[20] If you looked down one side, for example, you would find the words "one," "light," "up," "hot," "right," "good." The other side then yields "many," "dark," "down," "cold," "left," "bad." Guess in which column you would find "male" and in which "female"?[21] As I have remarked before, people tend to see the cosmos in terms of their own social arrangements.

Now, it is possible to make a modern list of pairs of opposites. These will of course be different from the Greek ones, although some of the ancient opposites still have power to puzzle us. The opposition between individual and society (the one versus the many), for example, has always remained an obsession in the West. We still almost inevitably perceive things in terms of sameness and difference, and we love pointing to the ancient notion of an abyss between the rational and the emotional. Today we often take to be self-evident the opposition between science and culture, the secular and the religious, individual values and morality, reason and imagination, objective and subjective, material and immaterial, practicality and inefficiency, useful and symbolic, novel and *vieux jeu*, knowledge and ignorance — the list could be lengthened considerably. Most of us can tell at once which column is supposed to be admirable and which less so, just as ancient Greeks knew that it was better to belong to the male, bright column than the female, dark one. Science, the new, reason, knowledge, the useful — who would want to be counted among those opposed? This column having been taken to be preferable, it is also, as a further step, assumed to be interlinked. And then it also comes about that imagination, religion, culture, the merely symbolic and subjective, the ignorant are all lumped together.

Our system of opposites, like that of the Greeks, is embodied in myths, such as that of the heroic technologist battling the forces of ignorance and uselessness, or the triumph of reason over what has had its day. I once described in these terms the dramatic and highly symbolic

conflict that occurred during much of the twentieth century between margarine and butter.[22] Margarine had all of
modernity on its side: technology, replaceability, unifor-
mity, predictability, efficiency, shelf life, and cheapness.
The people who grew oil-bearing plants for margarine-
making, and who did not traditionally eat fat spread on
bread, produced crops for export and could be paid little.
Butter, on the other hand, was relatively expensive, since
dairy farmers lived where butter is normally eaten and
were able to look after their own interests. Butter's myth
involved its uniqueness, its irreplaceable character
(though margarine was created to replace it), and its
occupying a quasi-moral "high ground" as both the natural and the original (that which margarine was trying to
imitate). Processed foods tend now to use margarine;
gourmets, meanwhile, continue to prize butter for its inef-
fable and still-inimitable culinary qualities. Pastry, no
matter what sort of fat it contains, has yet to be advertised
as "margariny."

The fast-food empire is at present under scrutiny for
reasons that include politics and obesity.[23] Fast food fights
back against its detractors by claiming on its side popu-
larity, convenience, predictability, and, again, apparent
cheapness. It wants elitist, expensive, unusual gourmet
food to be perceived as its opposite. But fast food is cheap
only in a very specific sense: that of its price at the point of
purchase. It is certainly not cheap when its destructive
side-effects, ecological, political, and nutritional, are
taken into account. Furthermore, to oppose the fast and
the gourmet is to disguise the fact that the truly important

war zone is everyday food, eaten at home. The issues that really demand to be resolved include people's power over their food supply, its cost, and its quality, together with questions of time allocation and the skills that make for human responsibility and independence.

Fast food versus gourmet food is a fake battle, a diversionary skirmish to distract attention from what is really going on. Dualism is like a fatal diagram: it can prevent us from seeing what is in fact important, what the other possibilities are. It may also be cynically wielded to prevent effective opposition to a specific plan of action. It can remove in advance the ability to imagine a different picture of the way things are. Take, for example, pluralism, relativism, and the inarguability of individual values: my values are mine, and yours are yours; the truth is quite literally neither here nor there. Let us call to mind again the system of *moirai*, the boundaries between different fates; it was *hybris* to invade one's neighbour's *moira*. The very same picture describes modern relativism, the boundaries around the flat areas of each value system, every one of them of unassailable worth. Polite acceptance of my neighbour's views no matter what they are becomes a virtue, admired as the avoidance of *hybris*. It is not rocking the boat but upholding the status quo. It means denying that there is any truth that transcends the diagram of *moirai*. But where there is no transcendent truth, there is in fact no freedom.

The picture is misleading. It imposes itself, however, because it depicts one of our few remaining moral ideals: a lively and indeed admirable demand for at least formal respect for each person from every other. We have seen that the fatal diagram, rooted ultimately as it always is in honour and shame, should now apply mainly to systems of taste and good manners, social rules that have at best a quasi-moral nature. But the diagram, once it has been accepted because of one useful aspect, implies more: that thought itself comes in watertight parcels "protected" by boundaries; that beliefs are immobile, unshared — and unshareable. The facts, of course, are that ideas do travel — more satisfactorily, indeed, than commodities do. Cultures influence one another — they develop, change, converge — and on the other hand, people are always capable of choosing to dissociate themselves from ambient ways of thinking. Every human being understands what injustice is, especially when he or she experiences it. Therefore, despite the protests of relativists, an idea like that of human rights *can* be understood by absolutely everybody.

However, we are offered another inherently diagrammatical model, a way of picturing the way things are today. Again the image is a circle or a sphere, but this time the circle is empty; it is not composed of interlocking, independent *moirai* snug within the outline that is necessity. The name we have chosen for this schema is globalization. We couldn't call it by a term deriving from "total"; "totalitarianism" had already been taken. Latin languages try words like *mondialisation*, but they find it hard to resist: "globalization" includes in it the word "globe," the perfectly spherical picture of both world and fate. The world is one, is what globalization says, and it lies open, like an arena; no walls protect the various areas within it. There is no alternative, no escape, and no point in trying to make it different from what it is.

An important difference between these two pictures of the world is that the empty circle — everything is up for grabs — is for thinking about commerce and consumerism, while the mosaic that is relativism is for ideas. *Mere* ideas, I should say, for if we were to locate globalization and relativism in the two modern columns of opposites, globalization as an image would be ranked with science, efficiency, business, rationality, objectivity, and the rest, while relativism serves to immobilize — in the name of protecting — opinions, religions, cultures (the word, as I have said, is, significantly, now plural), feelings, and so on. Relativism, for all its inbuilt haziness as a concept, can easily contribute to fatalistic thinking; fatalism can be a very useful context in which highly organized groups can operate to their own advantage. Liberty, for each person, is thought to come from keeping beliefs to oneself, as part of private life. But in fact, the market is what is left free — to present itself as the one controlling value. Relativism encourages social disengagement and fragmentation, the disappearance of meaningful politics, the avoidance of discussion, no change, no movement. It divides, making it easier for something like globalization to rule.

Globalization and relativism may also be understood as a pair of opposites linked to movement and to immobility, respectively. Movement, in this schema, has been appropriated by globalization. (Ancient Greeks thought

of the circumference of a circle as the expression of movement itself: high, bright, light, and swift like the sun, in
opposition to the dark and stationary centre, which for
them was the earth.) Business class in airplanes and business lounges in airports are for the new aristocracy, those
in all but constant flight around the world, promoting
and ensuring the global reach of commerce. Once a place
or a resource has been exploited, money moves on. If
threatened by laws or by protest, money moves out.
Poverty is now, almost by definition, immobile; the
exploited are those who remain to pick up the pieces, if
there are any left to retrieve. The only mobility for the
poor is likely to consist of desperate journeys undertaken
in the hope of escape.[24] This arrangement sees globalization as one and moving, while ideas and most people are
many and static, and of course unable to get a purchase
on what is happening to them, let alone to catch up or
fight back. Globalization and relativism, backed up by
their two diagrammatic representations, become two
aspects of fate, active and passive. As a team they
behave like a pair of pincers, able to command helpless
acquiescence: a feeling, among those being milked and
manipulated, that nothing can be done to alter the plot.

Where people believe in fate, they feel that what happens could not have been otherwise. There is a special
satisfaction about fatal outcomes in fiction. The characters
in a story are not in charge; it is the author who devises
the plot. The pattern drives the action; it is fate. Fiction is
therefore different from life, where people live their own
lives, contending with circumstances and accidents with-

out being totally determined by them. Fate, which gives a story a separate existence from the characters in it, turns back upon itself like a line tying a knot in itself — or a knot being untied, as in the French term *dénouement*. The plot works itself out like a ticking bomb. In any case, the end and the beginning are so interdependent that effects appear to have given rise to causes. The metaphors of chance, on the other hand, express non-systematic meaninglessness: nothing connects up with anything else; there is no reason to do one thing rather than another.

An important deficiency of the fatal diagram, therefore, is its failure to describe meaning without distorting it, while recourse to chance ends up denying its existence. Meaning is therefore part of the way out of believing in fate. Meaning resides where direction is neither overwhelming nor totally lacking — in much the same way that individual personhood is truly respected only where the group is regarded as neither inevitably overriding nor non-existent. Meaning requires the work of a living human being: meaning has to be meant.

The English verb "to mean" is from *maenan*, to tell. It means "to have in mind" with an intention of communicating; its sense, therefore, is both "to signify" and "to intend." A person requires something outside the self to move towards or intend. The nouns "meaning" and "sense" imply both a direction and a goal. The French word *sens*, which signifies both direction and meaning, expresses the connection perfectly. Human beings have an inborn desire for meaning; our innate capacity for speech is both symptom and engine of this demand.

Connection is another attribute of meaning: a natural human reaction to seeing a crowd of dots is to seek a pattern in them, even to join them up and make pictures of them so that they "make sense," as in the signs of the zodiac. Human thinking is patterned; that is why we like thinking with linear images — and also why we enjoy reading stories with patterned plots. And human memory requires both order and meaning. The metaphor of flying dots is inherently unsatisfying to us because it is an answer that denies meaning. It is nevertheless offered to us as modernity's answer to fatalism. But it remains on the flat level, the same level as that of its opposite, the fatal diagram. It represents a refusal of transcendence.

One of our differences from animals lies in the complexity of our speech and its concomitant requirement of meaning; we are conscious in a manner that animals are not. This consciousness and desire for meaning is the beginning of an endless and disinterested quest to know and understand. And this in itself provides the possibility of distance from our own projected images so that we can free ourselves from their errors and inadequacies. The first thing we need to do to escape from fatalism is to insist on this distance, to rise higher than both the diagram and the meaningless space outside it, so that we can see where the image helps and where it is fallacious.

The diagram is quite good at depicting aspects of the way things are, otherwise it would not be useful. It is helpful for counting and measuring — and ours is a culture that obsessively validates the quantitative. It handily illustrates force operating in society: pressure, transgression, laws, law-breaking, and punishment. We have seen that it can also depict the immunities offered by human rights. But being a diagram, it is only two-dimensional, an abstraction. It politely leaves the areas within its lines empty — as empty as the vacancy outside the picture. It cannot give us human beings, and it shows only artificially isolated aspects of human life. It cannot express aspiration or indeed emotion, anger or love. The image can express revenge; it cannot speak of forgiveness. Freedom appears only as either immunity or escape. It cannot explain human desires and intellectual demands for something higher and bigger than nature (spatial though the metaphors remain).

Nature contains no justice — yet human beings long for it. We also cannot refrain from asking why the world exists, and the world cannot account for itself. To say that the world — or fate — "just is," or that "the laws of physics are eternal,"[25] either explains nothing or begs further questions. Science itself depends upon a deep faith that there *are* explanations for the things it investigates, and moreover, that we are able to understand them. These are breathtaking assumptions. Yet we make them, and we expect them not to let us down. There is intelligibility in the universe: if any fact astounds us, that one should. All of us perceive a difference between what there is and what we would like there to be, what we know and what we experience as a need to find out. This gap the image cannot address, and it is we ourselves who supply the dissatisfaction.

We can also start releasing ourselves from the fetters

of fate if we go right back to the roots of the diagram and remind ourselves that the one dimension missing from it is that of time. The image, in representing time, replaces it; fatalistic thinking relies upon this substitution. Drawing a line describes time but infects it with some of the properties of space, such as that of remaining, whereas time passes. A closed outline is worse still: with it, time either becomes cyclic or all but disappears as the image turns into an explanation of immobile, and therefore fatal, "portions" of the dispositions of society at any given moment. Movement necessarily becomes transgression, a jostling for power in the form of "space." The simple line is better, in that at least there is movement on it; time's arrow gives it direction. The line splits, and there is choice: which line, which direction, should I take?

Modern science's immense and ongoing progress has replaced the static models previously accepted with a new dynamic view: essentially, modern science has found ways of reintroducing us to time. Evolution takes place in time and makes *probability* a principle of explanation. And the probable has become the "field" in which modern thinkers see us exercising choice. We are offered an area of choice; once a specific decision among all the possible others has been made, another span opens up with its own possibilities, and later another and another. Spatial metaphors have not released their grip — but time has returned to the picture, together with the possibility of change. The schema manages to combine both the continuing line and a series of areas.

Human beings remain limited, however, for each time

a fan of opportunities opens out, its parameters are evident: we cannot choose absolutely anything. But we *can choose*, and our decisions open up other choices later on. Probabilities — eventually — emerge. Statistics, despite the reifying effect they commonly have on our thinking, and despite the trivial ends to which they are usually put, have taught us a great deal about probabilities. In this way, they have helped to introduce into everyday thinking — and not only into theoretical discourse — the liberating concept of time. The possibility of a dynamic model is a massive and distinctively modern insight.

But still the model is flat, and the need for another dimension, a step not merely forwards but upwards, is urgent. It is as though "on and on" has come to preclude "up and up," much as the fatal diagram substitutes itself, if we are not very careful, for time. The terrible modern temptation is to change everything but ourselves — to seek any technological fix rather than a change of heart. I once heard a man at a conference lecturing about the ocean's tides. He spoke at length about the problems we have with tides — the damage they cause, the inconvenience, the expense. Finally, he said — and I thought at first he was joking, but he was not — that we *can* improve our lot and rid the earth of tides. We could eliminate the moon, he said — and proceeded to show that we have the means to do it.

That is an example of flat thinking — and it is every bit as modern as our dynamic new models of the way things are. It is narrowly fixated on seeking a "solution" to one problem without acknowledgement even of the possible consequences of such meddlesomeness. It shows, further, a lack of response, of respect, of any sense that, our own present and temporary interests notwithstanding, the moon is not ours to destroy. It is the sign — a frighteningly common one in our day — of a refusal to convert first of all the human will. As Samuel Johnson said, "He who has so little knowledge of human nature, as to seek happiness by changing any thing, but his own dispositions, will waste his life in fruitless efforts, and multiply the griefs which he purposes to remove."[26] Of course, the phrase "converting the human will" implies something to believe in, something to turn towards, a reason for action that lies beyond our own immediate self-interest.

The ecological movement is transcendental because it is prepared to set something — plants, animals, the earth as a whole — beyond our egotistical reach. It asks human beings to change their own attitudes of mind, or at least to give themselves pause, before setting out to fatten themselves through facile destruction. It admits something other than force, convenience, and money as an overriding principle. Similarly, acceptance of the points of view of the marginalized into mainstream society is an occasional modern instance of transcendental thinking: allowing people who lack power to be heard is far from natural, because it's far from considerations of material force. The feminist movement is a signal example of transcendence in modern society: it asks the powerful to give up some of their power in the name of truth and fairness.

Proponents of each of these examples, of course, are

able to show that turning towards something other than force in fact makes for human happiness. But proving it is a laborious undertaking: most people are difficult to convince, for the conversion of *ourselves* and doing what is right out of principle even if it should be costly are difficult ideals. "Rising" is a good metaphor for such attitudes of mind, not only because a higher vantage point enables us to see more, but also because rising implies fighting the force of gravity. People who rise in this fashion require a real commitment to the new, as opposed to the ersatz newness known as novelty that is offered us by technology. For the newness in question lies above and beyond the way things recently have been and mostly still are.

Transcendence is achieved today in the face of enormous opposition. It always has been hard to achieve, of course, but people once paid it at least lip service. Today it is a concept that has become so improper as to be almost unmentionable. This has not made it easier to explain why selfishness is destructive of oneself as well as of others; why we should control a thirst for revenge and seek understanding and reconciliation rather than use our might to make people pay; or even why it might be wiser to put up with tides and keep the moon. What has caused this rejection to come about? I want to return to our fatal diagram for one last time, with honour and shame enforcing the fated lines inside the picture and escape from fate into chance outside its outline.

We tend today to experience shame in a diluted form, as what we call embarrassment. (The dilution probably occurred because we are heirs to a religious tradition that is steadfastly opposed to shame in the sense in which I have used the word in this book.) The term "embarrassment" derives from the Spanish *embarazar*, to hinder by placing a bar or impediment in the way. Shame, in a culture like that of ancient Greece, was among other things a preventive mechanism, what made a person decide not to do the wrong thing. It was experienced as the pressure of the opinion of others, the weight of society's predetermined preferences. Today we feel embarrassment most often when an inadequacy either is revealed or threatens to be uncovered (clothing, significantly, is a common source of this minor version of shame), or when there is a failure to behave in the manner prescribed.[27] Embarrassment's main effect is to inhibit; it instils reluctance. A person embarrassed is always uneasily aware of the judgement of other people, or the possibility of their disapproval, because of a social impropriety he or she has committed or might conceivably commit. It is a matter of *propriety*, of prestige, and of image; morality is rarely the point.

The choices people confront today often include, as we have seen, simple-minded lists of opposites. These pairs of opposites are set out by society in advance. They come not only linked by being listed in columns but also bristling with possibilities for approval or for contempt. The choice that ought to be made in these cases is mostly very clear; the penalty for coming down on the wrong side will most probably suggest that one is making all the other wrong choices as well. Embarrassment, or even outright intimidation, will strive to prevent such disobedience from occurring.[28] This mechanism is in itself regrettable, and indeed there is nothing new about it. Ideally, people should always be prepared to judge and to choose because of the merits of the case in hand, and not because of social pressures. In our society, after all, we still do not have to live in fear of physical persecution if we hold opinions that disagree with a model in vogue.

Far more serious is the unexamined nature of the oppositions themselves. Religious faith, for example, is thoughtlessly dismissed as inimical to science, whereas it is at least as likely that, in the words of the Canadian theologian Bernard Lonergan, "the affirmation of God and the search of intellect for faith arise out of a sincere acceptance of scientific presuppositions and precepts."[29] Subjectivity and feeling are presumed to be inferior to objectivity and reason. But how do we know that the "reason" in question is "objective" (exactly why was this man excited by his idea of blowing up the moon?), and why should feelings be discounted? What happens, as the anthropologist Mary Douglas has shown in her book *Missing Persons*,[30] is that a model of the way things are is constructed, then anything that does not fit the model is thrown out, and finally a different model comes to seem inconceivable. The result is the quasi-deliberate entertainment of what she calls "patches of ignorance." There follows a refusal to investigate, a prevention of discussion, then blindness, trivialization, and a disastrous narrowing of consciousness.

For example, the prestige — and the monetary

rewards — of a specific practical project may pressure a scientist to turn away from a purely scientific desire to know. Embarrassment was often, originally, a financial condition (a person unable to pay was said to be "financially embarrassed"). Given a culture where both prestige and value are synonymous with money, embarrassment can still take the form of *not being paid*. Similarly, the fact that other people might despise anything suggesting a belief in God should not — but often does — cause a turning away, in embarrassment, from even the possibility of self-transcendence. Embarrassment is a desire not to get involved with something either outside one's experience or too demanding — particularly if it involves emotional effort, and if there is no reward of honour, or at least approval, from others.

Now, if embarrassment is a limited and diluted modern version of shame as an inhibition, what, in our society, energizes us, propels us to act as society prefers, as honour does in an honour-and-shame system? We do honour, in a relatively small degree, people of whose behaviour we approve, but here I am talking about pressure before such behaviour occurs. What makes us obey in the first place? I believe that in our world, this energizing role is played by boredom.

Boredom, in its present form, is an entirely modern concept. It arrived as a fully-fledged attitude in western Europe with the eighteenth-century Enlightenment. The word "bored," appearing first in English in 1766, meant literally "attacked as with a drill to the head." Boredom is an irritable condition, and it demands alleviation *right now*. (It is utterly unlike ancient psychic states such as *acedia*, a sort of torpid apathy, or the romantic languors of *ennui* and *spleen*. Melancholia, or depression, is also a modern epidemic, but it lacks boredom's prodding quality.[31]) Boredom is a feeling of fury reacting to repetitiveness, or alternatively a sense of emptiness, of finding nothing worth doing, let alone striving for; it is the experience of dullness and generalized meaninglessness. Where embarrassment corresponds to the fatal diagram we have been discussing in that it protects closed systems or ideologies and abhors both change and involvement, boredom is about what we called dots: not a diagram but rather featureless space, futile movement, meaningless inconsequence.

Boredom is the motivating force of a consumer society. Bored people buy stuff for temporary relief from their condition. Feeling flat? Let me offer you a car, a pair of shoes, a cruise. Distract yourself: you'll forget about your boredom for a while — until, obligingly, you require relief once more. Boredom is not only a result but a *sine qua non* of consumerism. It is part of a social pattern, even a strategy: it gives rise to activity in and for itself, providing a counterpart to the refusal of alternatives ensured by embarrassment.

There are occasions when boredom is thought insufficient as a propellant, and addiction is suggested instead; a great many advertisements playfully tell us that we are, or should become, addicted. This is a metaphor, of course, when it is applied to chocolates or watching football or driving a particular kind of car.

Addiction, in such advertising, is an attempt to introduce, as it were, a line among the dots: addicted persons
will want one particular thing — the advertised thing —
repeatedly. It is an understandable commercial fantasy.
Real addiction can, of course, enter the picture at any
point: addiction to shopping, for instance, to the point of
kleptomania. I said before that ours is not a permissive
society but an addicted society. Neither boredom nor
addictions have anything to do with freedom. Boredom
is also an offshoot of the massive modern backing of efficiency, which so often turns work into regimented and
uninteresting routines. It arises out of loneliness and
lack of connection, not only with other people but also
with ourselves. It is above all a result of the destruction
of meaning.

Boredom and embarrassment are demons specific to
people who are in the main free from material risk. Our
society, relative to most other societies on earth, is rich
enough to contain many people who say they "live to
shop" and really believe it. They don't want anything in
particular; they only want something to buy, and money
with which to buy something — almost anything. Shopping becomes entertainment, vitality, even identity and
self-worth. They live in that distracted but willing and
docile state that makes, in a consumer society, an ideal cit-
izen. Boredom on the one hand and embarrassment on
the other — shadows as they are of honour and shame —
assist the slide into fatalism. They help to prevent vitality
in politics; they cause people to avoid thinking, to ignore
anything that does not lie at surface level; they work to

ensure that what Charles Taylor, the philosopher, calls "moral sources" remain inarticulate.

Escape from fatalism and its twin warders, boredom and embarrassment, begins simply with consciousness — with paying attention. To be disinterested — that is, to be interested in things in and for themselves, and not because of possible profits for yourself — and especially to pay attention to what is supposed to be boring or taken for granted, is to begin to effect a minor revolution, another word for which is "conversion." Notice immediately that paying attention is an *action*: we are free to do it — or to turn away. The next step is to concentrate — deliberately bring to bear all one's intelligence — on what needs to be understood. Then comes questioning — endless checking and unrestricted questioning, which involves mastering fear both of change in oneself and of other people's disapproval. Higher still (higher, not lower) comes response, both affective and practical, to what has been discovered: something is felt, and something must be done. Each step entails a free choice, a turning towards what is important, what entails and explains everything else, what really matters; it implies a turning away from distractions and comfortable errors, the traps of fate.

There is an abyss between knowing what one should do and actually doing it. This divide can be crossed only by each person, personally. The step is made in freedom: it is always possible to know what to do and not to do it. *Willingness* is involved, just as openness and readiness are requirements for insight, or indeed for any spiritual experience. All of the stages imply conversion, especially conversion of the will.

The four steps I have just described constitute what Bernard Lonergan called the Transcendental Precepts. They are stages and levels on a journey upwards and out of flat fatalism: Be attentive; Be intelligent; Be reasonable (for one can be very intelligent and still lack the humility to be reasonable); Be responsible. Later, he described a higher level still — that of love of God, of all humanity, of all of nature.[32] "Be in love" is Lonergan's fifth Transcendental Precept.

Human minds naturally want to know; they spontaneously reach for answers to questions. But those questions, if we are not vigilant, can be stifled, ignored, drowned out. We are free to search — and free to give up, to get distracted, to remain ignorant. We are persons — that is, subjects, not objects. We contend with various givens — our physical constitutions, the society of people we live with, the natural environment. But we are free to choose what to do both within and with respect to that context, how to feel and how to react in every moment of time. We are not enthralled to fate as something separate from ourselves, a road we are forced willy-nilly to follow. We can consciously stand apart, even from something as deeply ingrained in us as is the fatal diagram. We can coolly look it over and see what it illuminates, what it obfuscates, and above all what it leaves out. If we understand it, judge its usefulness, take note of its limitations, we can move beyond fate — if such be our desire and our will.

NOTES

Chapter I: Drawing a Line

1   See further, Margaret Visser, *Much Depends on Dinner* (Toronto: McClelland and Stewart, 1986), pp. 133–36.

2   Charles Darwin, *On the Origin of Species by Means of Natural Selection, or the Preservation of Favoured Races in the Struggle for Life*, 6th ed. (London: John Murray, 1882; first published 1872), pp. 49, 63, 65, 70. See further, Hilary Rose, "Colonising the Social Sciences?" in Hilary Rose and Stephen Rose, eds., *Alas, Poor Darwin* (London: Cape, 2000), pp. 106–28.

3   Darwin later complained that he was being said to have "proved 'might is right,' and therefore that Napoleon is right, and every cheating tradesman is also right." Despite his appropriation of Spencer's phrase, Darwin expressed admiration for the human desire and ability to "oppose natural selection" through helping the weak. See further, Marshall Sahlins, *The Use and Abuse of Biology* (London: Tavistock, 1977), especially part 3, "Biology and Ideology,"

where Darwin's letter is cited on p. 103. See also Richard Hofstadter, *Social Darwinism in American Thought* (New York: Braziller, 1959).

4   In a letter to Engels, Marx wrote: "It is remarkable how Darwin recognises among beasts and plants his English society with its division of labour, competition, opening up of new markets, single 'inventions,' and the Malthusian 'struggle for existence.'" Karl Marx and Friedrich Engels, *Selected Correspondence 1846–1895*, 9th ed. (London: Lawrence and Wishart, 1943), pp. 125–26. Cited in Rose, *Alas, Poor Darwin*, p. 111. See further, Alfred Schmidt, *The Concept of Nature in Marx* (London: NLB, 1971).

5   William Shakespeare, *As You Like It*, Act 2, scene 1, lines 15–17.

6   Ludwig Wittgenstein, *The Blue and Brown Books* (Oxford: Basil Blackwell, 1958), pp. 107–09.

7   Lewis Carroll, *Through the Looking-Glass and What Alice Found There* (1896), chapter 5. See Martin Gardner, *More Annotated Alice* (New York: Random House, 1990), p. 234.

8   The last lines of Robert Frost's poem "The Road Not Taken" (1916) are:

> Two roads diverged in a wood, and I —
> I took the one less traveled by,
> And that has made all the difference.

9   See Wayland D. Hand, "Boundaries, Portals, and Other Magical Spots in Folklore," *Catherine Briggs Lecture* 2 (November 1982); Martin Puhvel, *The Crossroads in Folklore and Myth* (New York: Peter Lang, 1989).

10 Sophocles, *Oedipus Tyrannus*, lines 794–813, 715–16, and *passim*.

11 This pottery style dates from ca. 1050 B.C. to 700 B.C.

12 The ancient Greek philosopher Heraclitus was of the opinion, similar in important respects to that of Shakespeare, that "a man's character is his daimon." (H. Diels and W. Kranz, *Die Fragmente der Vorsokratiker* [hereafter referred to as DK], 6th ed. [Berlin, 1952], 22 B 119.) A daimon was a demi-god who caused fate to be fulfilled. Shakespeare, as a Christian, insists upon free will in human beings, although he uses the rich tradition of fatalism in fiction, a subject I shall discuss in chapter 2.

13 For example, the birth of Peleus (*Iliad*, Book xxiv, line 534) and his wedding to Thetis (a favourite subject of Greek vase paintings; described in Catullus 64, lines 320f.).

14 In a modern philosophical account of time, we find the following statements: "The space inside individuals is different from the space surrounding them. . . . Still, the space inside individuals is the same as the space outside them. How shall we interpret the difference so that it is a difference of the spaces themselves? The answer, though tinged with metaphor, is that the space inside an individual is thicker or more intense than the space outside of it." Irwin C. Lieb, *Past, Present, and Future. A Philosophical Essay about Time* (Urbana and Chicago: University of Illinois Press, 1991), p. 70.

15 James Olney sums up this part of Jung's theory: "Unable to go out of himself to right or left, [man] can only transcend what he is by realizing the pattern from above or, which is the same thing, by tracing out the ground plan which exists *in potentia* when he is born." *Metaphors of Self* (Princeton, NJ: Princeton University Press, 1972), p. 49.

16 Carl Jung, "On Psychic Energy," *Collected Works*, R. F. C. Hall, trans. (Princeton, NJ: Princeton University Press, 1960), p. 33; c.f. p. 111.

In the opening lines of T. S. Eliot's *Four Quartets*, the reference to life's journey as a closed outline is clear:

Time present and time past
Are both perhaps present in time future
And time future contained in time past.

The final section of the last of the four poems begins with the words

We shall not cease from exploration
And the end of all our exploring
Will be to arrive where we started
And know the place for the first time.

17 Samuel Beckett, *Proust* (New York: Grove Press, 1957; first published 1931), p. 10.

18 See Norbert Elias, *The Civilizing Process*, vol. 1 (New York: Urizen, 1978; first published 1939).

19 Heraclitus, DK 22 B 103.

20 The Doomsday Book of 1086 is a description of the property in most of England at that time, for use in cases of litigation. The book is to do with boundaries and ownership, and "doom" here means judgement. The two ideas, legal judgement and boundaries, easily meet in one word — a word that came to mean fate.

21 John 8:32.

22 For more about these metaphors, see Margaret Visser, *The Geometry of Love* (Toronto: HarperCollins, 2000).

Chapter II: Fate and the Furies

1   Carl Gustav Jung, *Memories, Dreams, Reflections*, Aniela Jaffé, ed., Richard and Clara Winston, trans. (New York: Pantheon Books, 1963), pp. 87–88.

2   Ibid., p. 72.

3 Ibid., p. 109.

4 See Margaret Visser, *The Rituals of Dinner* (Toronto: HarperCollins, 1991), pp. 227–42.

5 See J. G. Peristiany, ed., *Honour and Shame: The Values of Mediterranean Society* (Chicago: University of Chicago Press, 1966), especially Julian Pitt-Rivers, "Honour and Social Status," pp. 21–77.

6 Homer, *Iliad*, Book XXII. For this particular point, see line 5.

7 The gods have parcelled out the universe among themselves: the *moira* of Zeus is the sky, of Poseidon the sea, of Hades the underworld; Gaia, who, like fate, was there first, is earth. Aphrodite has sexual love, Artemis has virginity, and so on.

8 Fates are given sizes, extensions in space, and in this common metaphor for fatal turning-points, heavinesses that can be "weighed in the balance."

9 A group of people may agree to proclaim their forgiveness — or to ask for pardon for what they have done as a group — but no group can vouch for what each of its members feels.

10 Elias, *Civilizing Process*.

11 Erasmus warned of this, even as he took manners seriously, in his enormously influential work on civility: *De civilitate morum puerilium libellus* (Froben, Bâle, 1530), trans. by B. McGregor, in *Literary and Educational Writings*, vol. 25 of *Collected Works of Erasmus*, J. K. Sowards, ed. (Toronto: University of Toronto Press, 1985).

12 See, for example, the Gospel of John 13:34–35 and St. Augustine's maxim "Love — then do what you will" (*In Epistolam Joannis*, tractatus 7, section 8). The meaning is that a person who really loves both God and other people will do his or her utmost to practise all the other virtues

as well.

13 For more on the subject of the requirement of authenticity in modern culture, see Charles Taylor, *Sources of the Self: The Making of the Modern Identity* (Cambridge: Cambridge University Press, 1989), especially part 5, and *The Malaise of Modernity* (Toronto: Anansi, 1991).

14 Aeschylus, *Eumenides*, part 3 of *The Oresteia*.

15 René Girard, *La Violence et le sacré* (Paris: Grasset, 1972); *Le Bouc émissaire* (Paris: Grasset, 1982); *Je vois Satan tomber comme l'éclair* (Paris: Grasset, 1999); *Celui par qui le scandale arrive* (Paris: Desclée de Brouwer, 2001). English translations are available of these and other books by Girard.

16 Paul Davies, "Before the Big Bang," *Prospect* (June 2001): 56–59.

17 See, for example, Olney, *Metaphors of Self*, p. 49.

18 For a clever and satirical exploration of the implications of diagrams, with creatures living in two dimensions, then one, then three, and finally four, see Edwin Abbott Abbott, *Flatland* (Princeton, NJ: Princeton University Press, 1991; first published 1884).

19 Heraclitus said that the sun himself would not leave his course around the earth because if he did the Furies, the handmaids of fate, would find him out (DK 22 B 94). The meaning of this magnificent paradox is that darkness in the economy of the physical universe is inseparable from, and so actually "supports," the light. The trajectory of the sun around the earth has become, for Heraclitus, *anangké*, the outline of the fatal diagram. There will be more about the presocratic philosophers and their division of the world into a series of opposites in chapter 5.

Chapter III: Free Fall

1   Simplicius, "Commentary on Aristotle's *Physics*," section 330.14ff.

2   Aelian, *On the Nature of Animals*, chapter 7, section 16.

3   For formality and informality in manners, see Margaret Visser, *The Rituals of Dinner*, *passim*.

4   DK 68 A 28. Anaxagoras had already been fascinated by motes in sunlight: DK 59 A 74.

5   DK 68 B 156. A good short account of Democritus and Atomism will be found in J. M. Robinson, *An Introduction to Early Greek Philosophy* (Boston: Houghton Mifflin, 1968), chapters 10 and 11. The history of Atomism from earliest times, including the subsequent developments of Epicurus, through the breakthroughs in science from the seventeenth century A.D. and on into the twentieth century, may be read in Andrew Van Melsen, *From Atomos to Atom* (Pittsburgh: Duquesne University Press, 1952); and Lancelot Law Whyte, *Essay on Atomism from Democritus to 1960* (London: Thomas Nelson, 1961).

6   DK 68 B 9; DK 68 A 49.

7   DK 68 B 164; DK 68 A 128.

8   DK 67 B 2; DK 68 A 68.

9   Rafaralahy Bemananjara, "A Touchstone of Time and Place," in *UNESCO: The Courier* (December 1984).

10   Compare the ancient Greek *klepsydra*: speakers in court were allowed to hold forth for as long as a certain amount of water took to run through a small hole.

11   My grandfather's clock was too large for the shelf,
     So it stood ninety years on the floor ...
     Ninety years without stumbling — tick tock, tick tock,

His life's seconds numbering, tick tock, tick tock —
But it stopped short — never to go again —
When the old man died.

Notice how in this song by Henry Clay Work, the grand-father's life was embodied by an object — his fate — separate from but remorselessly "applied" to himself.

12   The phrase is Henri Bergson's. See *An Introduction to Metaphysics*, T. E. Hulme, trans. (Indianapolis: Bobbs-Merrill, 1955; first published 1903); and *Time and Free Will*, F. L. Pogson, trans. (London: George Allen, 1913; first published 1889).

13   The word "railway," meaning tracks made first of wood, then of iron or steel, to smooth — and predetermine — the way for wagon wheels, was first used in 1756; the term predated the invention of the locomotive engine.

14   See Francis Mobio, "Stock-market Forecasting as Cosmography," *Diogenes* 48, no. 2 (2000): 43–57.

15   The idea of a "window of time" being "allotted" resembles a series of metaphors for time as space that the ancient Greeks derived from weaving thread into cloth. They used a loom that opened among the warp threads a space through which the shuttle bearing the woof had to pass at precisely the right moment, neither too early nor too late. This moment, this space, the Greeks called *kairos*. See R. B. Onians, *The Origins of European Thought* (Cambridge: Cambridge University Press, 1951), pp. 343–48.

16   See Bryan S. Turner, *For Weber: Essays on the Sociology of Fate* (London: Routledge and Kegan Paul, 1981), especially pp. 110, 176.

17   Robots have ancestors, notably in the clay golem of six-teenth- and seventeenth-century Prague. But the word seems first to have been invented by Karel Čapek in his

science-fiction drama *R.U.R.* (Rossum's Universal Robots) (London: Oxford University Press, 1947; first published in English 1923).

18 Hervé Kempf, *La Révolution biolithique: Humains artificiels et machines animées* (Paris: Albin Michel, 1998).

Chapter IV: Transgression

1 For more on this subject, see Visser, *The Geometry of Love.*

2 This idea is expressed with great eloquence by the theologian Bernard Lonergan in *Insight: A Study of Human Understanding*, Frederick E. Crowe and Robert M. Doran, eds. (Toronto: University of Toronto Press, 1992; first published 1957), pp. 372–76, 661–62, etc. "The immanent source of transcendence in man," wrote Lonergan, "is his detached, disinterested, unrestricted desire to know" (p. 659).

3 An exception is Aristotle, who could say, "The present inquiry does not aim at knowledge (*theoria*) as other inquiries did. Its purpose is not to know what virtue is, but to make ourselves good." *Nicomachean Ethics*, 1103 b 26.

4 See Plutarch, *On Talkativeness*, 511 B; *The E at Delphi*, 385 D; *The Dinner of the Seven Wise Men*, 164 B; Plato, *Protagoras*, 343 B; etc.

5 It was a "zero sum game." The phrase comes from mathematics, economics, and political theory, and it was first used by J. Von Neumann and Oskar Morgenstern, *Theory of Games and Economic Behavior* (Princeton, NJ: Princeton University Press, 1944). The idea itself is in Adam Smith (1723–1790).

6 Anaximander, DK 12 B 1; Hesiod, *Theogony*, 176–210, 453–506.

7 Livy, *Ab urbe condita*, book 1, chapter 54.

8   A. A. Milne, "Lines and Squares," in *When We Were Very Young* (London: Methuen, 1924.; first published 1921).

9   Hesiod, *Works and Days*, lines 202–12.

10   *"Il faut que je vive!" "Je n'en vois pas la nécessité."* Voltaire, *Alzire* (1736), "Discours Préliminaire" in *Oeuvres Complètes Théâtre*, vol. 2 (1877), p. 381.

11   See Michael Ignatieff, *The Rights Revolution* (Toronto: Anansi, 2000).

12   For differing opinions on human rights, from various cultures, see the articles in Paul Ricoeur, ed., *Philosophical Foundations of Human Rights* (Paris: UNESCO, 1986).

13   *"La notion d'obligation prime celle de droit, qui lui est subordonnée et relative."* Simone Weil, *L'Enracinement: Prélude à une déclaration des devoirs envers l'être humain* (Paris: Gallimard, 1949), opening sentence.

14   For more on this subject, see Margaret Visser, "Worship Your Enemy: Aspects of the Cult of Heroes in Ancient Greece," *Harvard Theological Review* 75 (1982): 403–28.

15   See further, Visser, *The Geometry of Love*, pp. 245–49.

Chapter v: Beyond Fate

1   Alfred Tennyson, *In Memoriam* (London: Blackie & Son, n.d., written 1833–50), verse LV. "The Hideous 'No' of Nature" is the title given to this section of Tennyson's poem by his editor, F. W. Robertson.

2   Richard Dawkins, *River Out of Eden* (London: Weidenfeld and Nicolson, 1995). I have taken this quotation from Dawkins's reading of his book on tape.

3   Chance is often shown in Greek literature to be merely a mask for fate. See, for example, *Oedipus Tyrannus*, where this is a central theme.

4 For much of what follows, see Evelyn Fox Keller, *The Century of the Gene* (Cambridge, MA: Harvard University Press, 2000). See also Bryan Appleyard, *Brave New Worlds: Genetics and the Human Experience* (London: HarperCollins, 2000).

5 Richard Dawkins, *The Selfish Gene* (Oxford: Oxford University Press, 1976).

6 James D. Watson, "The Meaning of the Genome," *Prospect* (October 2000) (Round table discussion).

7 Jean-Claude Guillebaud, *Le principe d'humanité* (Paris: Seuil, 2001), p. 202. See further, Daniel Altman, "Genetics and Insurance," *Prospect* (April 2001), pp. 56–59.

8 Guillebaud, *Le principe d'humanité*, p. 232.

9 S. Connor, "'Perfect Husband' Gene Discovered," *Independent*, 18 August 1999.

10 Walter Gilbert, "Vision of the Grail," in D. J. Kevles and L. Hood, eds., *The Code of Codes* (Cambridge, MA: Harvard University Press, 1992), pp. 83–97.

11 *Iliad*, Book IX, lines 565–72; Ovid, *Metamorphoses*, Book VIII, 451–525. Ancient Greek myths make women prefer their brothers to their sons. See Visser, "Medea," n. 21, below.

12 *Odyssey*, Book VII, 196–98, etc.; *The Library* of Apollodorus, Book III, 4.2, 6.2, 7.5, etc.; Aeschylus, *Seven Against Thebes*, 422–56; Euripides, *Phoenician Women*, 1172–86, and *Suppliants*, 496–99.

13 Some unique human abilities are speech, reason, abstraction, transmission of knowledge, partial control of instincts and needs, and imagination. To take behaviour to do with food as an example, human beings are the only animals to cook their food before eating it, and to share it and consume it while observing intricate and meaningful

systems of manners. (See Visser, *The Rituals of Dinner*.) Most important for the subject of this book, human beings are (uniquely) free, and are able to make choices based on ethical considerations.

14 Steve Jones, geneticist, "The Meaning of the Genome," *Prospect* (October 2000) (Round table discussion).

15 Aristotle, *Metaphysics* i, 5, 986 a 23.

16 Hippolytus, *Refutation of All Heresies*, ix 10, DK 22 B 60.

17 Hippolytus, *Refutation of All Heresies*, ix 10, DK 22 B 61.

18 Plotinus, *Enneads* iv, 8, 1. DK 22 B 84a.

19 Simplicius, *Commentary on Aristotle's* Physics, 145, 23; 146, 10. DK 28 B 8, 22–25 and 36–41.

20 Greeks themselves sometimes expressed an awareness that one column was "better" than the other. See, for example, the Scholion to Parmenides, DK 28 B 8, 56–59: "[F]ire is called the rare, the hot, the illumining, the soft, and the light, while the dense is called the cold, darkness, harsh, and heavy."

21 The power of Euripides' tragedy *Medea* depends in part on the scrambling, in a manner fiendishly confusing and terrifying for a Greek, of at least four of the pairs of opposites (male and female, motion and stillness, light and dark, and of course, honour and shame) — as well as the heroic pattern itself. See Margaret Visser, "Medea: Daughter, Sister, Wife and Mother: Natal Family versus Conjugal Family in Greek and Roman Myths about Women," in Martin Cropp, Elaine Fantham, and S. E. Scully, eds., *Greek Tragedy and Its Legacy: Essays Presented to D. J. Conacher* (Calgary: University of Calgary Press, 1986), pp. 149–65.

22 Visser, "Margarine: A Melodrama in Several Acts," in *Much Depends on Dinner*, pp. 102–14.

23 Eric Schlosser, *Fast Food Nation: What the All-American Meal*

Is Doing to the World (London: Allen Lane, The Penguin Press, 2001).

24 An extended reflection on this idea will be found in Zygmunt Bauman, *Globalization: The Human Consequences* (New York: Columbia University Press, 1998). See further, Jeremy Harding, *The Uninvited. Refugees at the Rich Man's Gate* (London: Profile Books, 2000).

25 See Dawkins, *River Out of Eden*, and Davies, "Before the Big Bang."

26 Samuel Johnson, the sixth *Rambler*. *The Works of Samuel Johnson*, vol. 1 (Troy, NY: Pafracts Book Company, 1903), p. 38.

27 For the mechanics of embarrassment, see Margaret Visser, *The Way We Are* (Toronto: HarperCollins, 1994), pp. 47–51, 98–106.

28 Jean-Paul Sartre, for example, used his considerable intellectual clout to condemn as "dogs" people who did not join him in admiring Communism (*"Tout anti-communiste est un chien"*). To express as a fatality the eventual triumph of Marxism, Sartre used a linear metaphor: "*Le marxisme est l'horizon indépassable de l'Histoire.*" Cited in Guillebaud, *La Refondation du monde* (Paris: Seuil, 1999), p. 100.

29 Lonergan, *Insight*, p. 765.

30 Mary Douglas and Steven Ney, *Missing Persons: A Critique of the Social Sciences* (Berkeley, CA: University of California Press, Russell Sage Foundation, 1998), p. 74.

31 See further, Patrick O'Farrell, *Boredom as Historical Motivation* (London: Quadrant, 1982), and R. Kuhn, *The Demon of Noontide: Ennui in Western Literature* (Princeton, NJ: Princeton University Press, 1976). See most vividly, Max Picard, *The Flight from God*, Marianne Kuschnitzky and J. M. Cameron, trans. (Washington, DC: Regnery Gateway,

1989; first published 1934).

32 Lonergan, *Insight*, and *Method in Theology* (Toronto: University of Toronto Press, 1990; first published 1971).

BIBLIOGRAPHY

Abbott Abbott, Edwin. *Flatland*. Princeton, NJ: Princeton University Press, 1991. First published 1884.

Bauman, Zygmunt. *Globalization: The Human Consequences*. New York: Columbia University Press, 1998.

Bergson, Henri. *Time and Free Will*. Translated by F. L. Pogson. London: George Allen, 1913. First published 1889.

Dietrich, B. C. *Death, Fate and the Gods*. London: Athlone Press, 1965.

Douglas, Mary, and Steven Ney. *Missing Persons: A Critique of the Social Sciences*. Berkeley, CA: University of California Press, Russell Sage Foundation, 1998.

Elias, Norbert. *The Civilizing Process*. Vol. 1. Translated by E. Jephcott. New York: Urizen, 1978. First published 1939.

Freud, Sigmund. *The Interpretation of Dreams*. Translated by James Strachey. London: G. Allen and Unwin, 1955. First published 1900.

Girard, René. *Je vois Satan tomber comme l'éclair*. Paris, Grasset, 1999.

Greene, William Chase. *Moira: Fate, Good, and Evil in Greek Thought*. New York: Harper and Row, 1944.

Guillebaud, Jean-Claude. *La refondation du monde*. Paris: Seuil, 1999.

——. *Le principe d'humanité*. Paris: Seuil, 2001.

Hand, Wayland D. "Boundaries, Portals, and Other Magical Spots in Folklore." *Catherine Briggs Lecture* 2, November 1982.

Jung, Carl Gustav. "On Psychic Energy." In *Collected Works*, vol. 8. Edited by Michael Fordham and Herbert Read. Translated by R. F. C. Hall. Princeton NJ: Princeton University Press, 1960.

——. *Memories, Dreams, Reflections*. Recorded and edited by Aniela Jaffé. Translated by Richard and Clara Winston. New York: Pantheon Books, 1963.

Lieb, Irwin C. *Past, Present, and Future: A Philosophical Essay about Time*. Urbana and Chicago: University of Illinois Press, 1991.

Lonergan, Bernard J. F. *Insight: A Study of Human Understanding*. Edited by Frederick E. Crowe and Robert M. Doran. Toronto: University of Toronto Press, 1992. First published 1957.

—— *Method in Theology*. Toronto: University of Toronto Press, 1990. First published 1971.

MacIntyre, Alasdair. *After Virtue*. London: Duckworth, 1999. First published 1981.

Monod, Jacques. *Le hasard et la nécessité*. Paris: Seuil, 1970.

Oakeshott, Michael. *On Human Conduct*. Oxford: Clarendon Press, 1996. First published 1975.

Olney, James. *Metaphors of Self*. Princeton, NJ: Princeton University Press, 1972.

Onians, Richard Broxton. *The Origins of European Thought about the Body, the Mind, the Soul, the World, Time and Fate*. Cambridge: Cambridge University Press, 1988. First published 1951.

Peristiany, J. G., ed. *Honour and Shame: The Values of Mediterranean Society*. Chicago: University of Chicago Press, 1966.

Picard, Max. *The Flight from God*. Translated by Marianne Kuschnitzky and J. M. Cameron. Washington, D.C.: Regnery Gateway, 1989. First published 1934.

Postman, Neil. *Technopoly: The Surrender of Culture to Technology*. New York: Random House, 1993.

Puhvel, Martin. *The Crossroads in Folklore and Myth*. New York: Peter Lang, 1989.

Ricoeur, Paul, ed. *Philosophical Foundations of Human Rights*. Paris: UNESCO, 1986.

Robinson, J. M. *An Introduction to Early Greek Philosophy*. Boston: Houghton Mifflin, 1968.

Rose, Hilary, and Stephen Rose, eds. *Alas, Poor Darwin*. London: Cape, 2000.

Sahlins, Marshall. *The Use and Abuse of Biology*. London: Tavistock, 1977.

Taylor, Charles. *Sources of the Self: The Making of the Modern Identity*. Cambridge: Cambridge University Press, 1989.

Turner, Bryan S. *For Weber: Essays on the Sociology of Fate*. London: Routledge and Kegan Paul, 1981.

Van Melsen, Andrew. *From Atomos to Atom*. Translated by H. J. Koren, Pittsburgh: Duquesne University Press, 1952.

Visser, Margaret. *The Geometry of Love*. Toronto: Harper-Collins, 2000.

———. *Much Depends on Dinner*. Toronto: HarperCollins, 2000. First published 1986.

———. *The Rituals of Dinner*. Toronto: HarperCollins, 2000. First published 1991.

———. *The Way We Are*. Toronto: HarperCollins, 2000. First published 1994.

———. "Worship your Enemy: Aspects of the Cult of Heroes in Ancient Greece." *Harvard Theological Review* 75 (1982): 403–28.

Whyte, Lancelot Law. *Essay on Atomism from Democritus to 1960*. London: Thomas Nelson, 1961.

INDEX

humility, 45–46, 93, 144
hybris, 94–101, 107, 109, 110, 114,
    121, 123, 127

ideals, 90–91, 93
ignorance, 77–78, 125, 139, 144
"image", 51, 112–113, 138
importance, 46, 77, 93, 95, 143
individual, individualism, 14,
    16–17, 24–25, 46–47, 49–50,
    53, 91;
  individual and group, 24, 25,
    125, 131;
  see also One and Many
informality, see formality
inherited guilt, 91
insight, 74, 108, 135, 143
intelligence, intelligibility, 93, 133,
    139, 143, 144
interiority, 46, 91
Internet, 75, 81
invasion, 49, 96–97, 99, 100, 101,
    107
IQ tests, 72

Johnson, Samuel, 136
journey, 9, 10, 20, 21, 24;
  see also road
Judaism, 21, 90
Jung, Carl Gustav, 13–14, 29–30,
    31, 147 n. 15
justice, 82, 89, 93, 103, 105,
    107–108, 115, 128, 133, 136

kairos, 152 n. 15
koros, 99

land, 14–15, 34–35, 97, 107;
  see also fences
language, 4–5, 6–7, 67, 68, 119,
    132
law, laws, 21–22, 25–26, 27–28,
    54–56, 91, 101, 102, 104, 115,
    130, 133;
  laws of nature, 122;
  laws of physics, 56, 133
liberation, liberty, see freedom

limits, 61, 86, 95, 101, 106, 123,
    134–135;
  see also boundary, fences;
  limited goods, 36, 39, 80, 95, 96,
    107;
  limited time, 68, 78
lines, 35–36, 142;
  representing time, 5–8, 13–14,
    18–19, 20, 36, 134
  See also boundaries
litigation, 107
Livy, 99
Lonergan, Bernard, 139, 143–144,
    153 n. 2
lot, 14–15, 37
lottery, 61
love, 49–50, 53, 92, 116, 117, 144,
    149 n. 12
luck, 61

machines, see technology
madness, 61, 95, 98
mafia, 47, 53
male and female, 42, 52, 54, 97,
    123, 124, 125
manners, 17, 47–48, 63, 106, 128,
    138;
  see also table manners
map, 9–10, 95, 107
margarine and butter, 125–126
market, the, 3, 79–80, 81, 86, 129
Marx, Karl, 4, 80, 146 n. 4
meaning, 25, 30–31, 33, 66, 68, 70,
    71, 75, 118, 131–132
meaninglessness, 66–68, 74–79,
    81, 84, 87, 94, 95, 106, 113,
    117, 131–132, 134, 142
memory, 8, 33, 76, 110, 132
metaphors, 2, 4, 5, 24, 32, 68, 89,
    93–94, 102, 116, 117, 119, 134,
    137, 141–142
  See also diagram, and other
    individual metaphors
Milne, A.A., 100–101
moira, moirai, 35–36, 39, 40, 57, 70,
    91, 95–96, 101–102, 115, 118,
    120–121, 127, 128, 149 n. 7

The CBC Massey Lectures Series

Also available from House of Anansi Press in this prestigious series:

The Cult of Efficiency
Janice Gross Stein
0-88784-678-5
(p) $19.95 CDN $14.95 US

The Rights Revolution
Michael Ignatieff
0-88784-656-4
(p) $16.95 CDN $16.95 US

The Triumph of Narrative
Robert Fulford
0-88784-645-9 (p) $16.95

Becoming Human
Jean Vanier
0-88784-631-9 (p) $17.95

The Elsewhere Community
Hugh Kenner
0-88784-607-6 (p) $14.95

The Unconscious Civilization
John Ralston Saul
0-88784-586-X (p) $14.95

On the Eve of the Millennium
Conor Cruise O'Brien
0-88784-559-2 (p) $12.95

Democracy on Trial
Jean Bethke Elshtain
0-88784-545-2 (p) $11.95

Twenty-First Century Capitalism
Robert Heilbroner
0-88784-534-7 (p) $11.95

The Malaise of Modernity
Charles Taylor
0-88784-520-7 (p) $14.95

Biology as Ideology
R. C. Lewontin
0-88784-518-5 (p) $11.95

Prisons We Choose to Live Inside
Doris Lessing
0-88784-521-5 (p) $9.95

Indefensible Weapons
Robert Jay Lifton and Richard Falk
0-88794-108-7 (p) $8.95

The Politics of the Family
R. D. Laing
0-88784-546-0 (p) $8.95

Nostalgia for the Absolute
George Steiner
0-88784-594-0 (p) $17.95

Necessary Illusions
Noam Chomsky
0-88784-574-6 (p) $24.95

Compassion and Solidarity
Gregory Baum
0-88784-532-0
(p) $11.95 CDN $11.95 US

The Real World of Democracy
C. B. Macpherson
0-88784-530-4
(p) $9.95 CDN $9.95 US

Latin America
Carlos Fuentes
0-88784-665-3 (p) $14.95

The Educated Imagination
Northrop Frye
0-88784-598-3 (p) $12.95

The Real World of Technology
Ursula Franklin
0-88784-636-X
(p) $16.95 CDN $11.95 US

Designing Freedom
Stafford Beer
0-88784-547-9 (p) $10.95